THE WORKPLACE

MANAGING

TODAY'S

DUAL-CAREER

FAMILIES

Cary L Cooper
AND
Suzan Lewis

KOGAN PAGE

First published in 1993

Apart from any fair dealing for the purposes of research or private study, or
criticism or review, as permitted under the Copyright, Designs and Patents
Act, 1988, this publication may only be reproduced, stored or transmitted, in
any form or by any means, with the prior permission in writing of the
publishers, or in the case of reprographic reproduction in accordance with
the terms of licences issued by the Copyright Licensing Agency. Enquiries
concerning reproduction outside those terms should be sent to the
publishers at the undermentioned address:

Kogan Page Limited
120 Pentonville Road
London N1 9JN

British Library Cataloguing in Publication Data

A CIP record for this book is available from the British Library.

ISBN 0 7494 1211 9

Typeset by DP Photosetting, Aylesbury, Bucks
Printed and bound in Great Britain by
Biddles Ltd, Guildford and King's Lynn

Contents

About the authors   8
Foreword   9

1 Introduction   11

The changing workforce   11
The dual-earner family   12
The traditional male work ethic   13
Why the workplace has to change   14

2 Stress and coping at work   19

Occupational stress and the male model of work   19
Work overload: long hours and the workaholic syndrome   22
Schedule incompatibility and inflexibility   24
Spillover   25
How do people cope?   28
How can organisations help?   33

3 Issues in career development   36

Preparing for a dual-career relationship   36
Parenting, careers and mobility   45
The stress of job mobility and relocation   50
How can organisations help?   54

4 Managing transitions: parenthood   57

The transition to parenthood   57
Dilemmas and issues for new parents   59
Informal policies: an example of good practice   68
Implications for organisations   70

5 Workers have families too   **74**

Time and energy   74
Conflicting demands   75
Effects on children   77
Childcare – who is responsible?   79
Who cares for the children when both parents are at work?   81
Who stays at home in a crisis?   84
Care of elderly parents and other relatives   87
What can organisations do?   88

6 Working together   **96**

Working together in the home   96
The concept of equity   100
Working together generating family income   102
Advantages of an egalitarian dual-career marriage   106
Men and women in organisations   108
How gender stereotypes cause misunderstandings at
    work   110
Sexuality and sexual harassment   112
What can organisations do?   114

7 Looking at alternatives   **119**

Alternative working arrangements   120
Reducing working hours   124
Easing the transition to parenthood   126

8 Training and development   **132**

Management training   132
Training which anticipates work/family issues   133
Skills for managing work and family   135
Conclusion   156

9 Changing organisations   **158**

Challenging the male model of work   159
Location and relocation   160
Opportunities for women   162
Wider societal changes and organisational policies   167

Childcare and social policy   171
Equal opportunities at work and at home   173

Appendix   *176*
Index   *180*

About the Authors

Cary L Cooper is currently Professor of Organisational Psychology and Deputy Chairman of the Manchester School of Management at the University of Manchester Institute of Science and Technology. He is the author of over 60 books (on stress, women at work and industrial and organisational psychology), has written over 250 articles for academic journals, and is a frequent contributor to national newspapers, TV and radio. He was founding President of the British Academy of Management, is currently Editor-in-Chief of the *Journal of Organizational Behavior*, and Fellow of the British Psychological Society and Royal Society of Arts.

Dr Suzan Lewis is a senior lecturer in psychology at Manchester Metropolitan University, where she is also co-director of the Elizabeth Gaskell Centre for Interpersonal and Organisational Development, a research, consultancy and training centre specialising in training and development for woman, and in the management of organisational change. She has written many articles and books on work and family issues and is co-editor of *Dual Earner Families: International Perspectives*, published by Sage, 1992. Her current research includes an evaluation of the impact of 'family friendly' employer initiatives on families and organisations.

Both authors are members of dual-career couples. Suzan Lewis is the mother of three sons and Cary Cooper has four children.

Foreword

Our first nanny was excellent. She was tidy around the house and developed a close, yet not too close, relationship with our eldest son, George. She stayed for two years, leaving only because she wanted a 'live-out' job, to allow her to share a flat nearby with her boyfriend.

We managed the transition carefully, avoiding tearful fare-wells, and quickly found a replacement. But we were anxious lest George should meet her in the neighbourhood, and be upset.

By pure mischance, they ran into each other in the local supermarket, three days after she left – she with her new charge, he with his new nanny. George waved a cheerful 'hello'; his former nanny burst into tears.

We recount this tale, not to demonstrate the hard-heartedness of our first-born, but to show that many of the preconceptions with which we began our career as ditkies (double income two kids) proved unfounded. Some children appear quite unfazed by regular changes in their childcare arrangements; others exhibit high anxiety. Sometimes, a dual-career structure seems positively advantageous, exposing children to a variety of influences and experiences they could not hope to match with one working parent; at other times the balancing act seems almost impossible.

Cooper and Lewis recognise that there are few absolutes in this rapidly-changing area. They accurately describe the tensions faced by dual-career couples, and raise pointed questions for couples themselves, and for their employers. Why do most dual-career families not practise the equal sharing they believe in? We can offer two, conflicting, answers to that question. Why have so few employers adapted their policies and practices, even though the evidence suggests that no company has suffered commer-cially from implementing effective equal opportunities policies?

Cooper and Lewis have explored these and other conundra, through their research with over 400 couples from those who, like us, can afford live-in help, to those for whom the cost of childcare is a vital criterion. The result is a fascinating exploration of the lifestyle and employment choices open to families and their employers, which personnel professionals, in particular, will find of great practical value.

Our own experience is, no doubt, untypical, but nonetheless worth recording. We have experienced stress. We have explored the outer reaches of the commuter marriage. (We have even considered taking out a contract on the head of Network SouthEast.) But we have still found the process of managing two careers and two children – which we began in our mid-30s – to be, ultimately, both rewarding and rejuvenating. As you review this cautionary catalogue of problems and poor practices, it might just be worth bearing that in mind.

Howard Davies, Director-General, CBI
Prudence Keely, Producer, BBC Question Time

1
Introduction

The nature of today's workforce is changing in important and fundamental ways. The growing numbers of men and women who are highly committed to their work and who also have a healthy commitment to and involvement in family and life beyond work are challenging organisations to rethink their most basis assumptions and practices. What we are witnessing is no less than a revolution in the workplace. As with all revolutions there has been some initial resistance, but the need to adapt to changing needs of the workforce is now widely recognised by successful organisations.

THE CHANGING WORKFORCE

The changing roles of men and women both at work and at home present new challenges to management. Economic need, smaller families and a shift to more egalitarian gender attitudes have all contributed towards the growing number of women in full-time employment. Women are increasingly entering what were previously considered male-dominated domains, including blue collar and skilled work, the professions and the field of management. However, unlike earlier generations of women, they are remaining in those careers after having children.

It is not only women's roles that are changing. Fewer men nowadays enjoy the support of a full-time homemaker wife to protect them from family work, and enable them to direct their energies exclusively towards their work. Women in dual-earner partnerships share the economic upkeep of the family and expect their partners to share the domestic and caring work. Increasingly, men want time to spend with their families and value time for care and involvement with children. They no longer want to be absentee fathers. Realising how much their own fathers missed, many of the younger generation of fathers have changed priorities. Careers remain an important source of identity for most people, but members of the new workforce are seeking balanced lives with involvement in both paid employment and family, where neither takes over their lives completely. If men and women are to achieve balanced lives and make an optimum contribution to their employing organisations, organisational structures, and especially managerial attitudes and behaviours, must adapt to their needs.

THE DUAL-EARNER FAMILY

The composition of the workforce has altered in a number of ways in recent decades. There are, for example, more single mothers, more members of ethnic minorities and more people with disabilities, in all fields of work, and all have special needs as well as offering special talents and contributions. The most significant change, however, is in the number of dual-earner, or dual-career couples. These are couples who deviate from the once traditional (and now minority) family pattern of male breadwinner and female homemaker. Both partners are (or wish to be) in paid employment and share the homemaker role, albeit rarely equally.

There are, of course, a number of different types of dual-earner families. Some remain relatively traditional, in that the man's career takes precedence and the woman plays a supportive role, adding paid employment to her household work. Others are more innovative. Their two careers are considered equally important, or the woman's career might take precedence over her partner's. Responsibility for children and household work may be shared equally, and in a minority of cases the man does most of this work. Most dual-earner families fall somewhere between the traditional and the non-traditional. While they may express egalitarian views, in practice the woman carries out most of the family work, often reluctantly. In some cases, the man feels guilty or uneasy about this gap between his ideals and the reality.

Why do most dual-earner families not practise the equal sharing they believe in? The reasons are complex, but include social pressures, the lower pay attaching to work primarily performed by women which reinforces the notion of the male as breadwinner and, particularly, managerial attitudes and the difficulty many men experience in trying to modify their involvement in paid work to make time for their family. Much of this stems from the traditional, male work ethic.

THE TRADITIONAL MALE WORK ETHIC

Since the Industrial Revolution it has been widely assumed that paid work is the province of a man, while the family is a woman's domain. Work has been organised around men who have had the support of a full-time housewife. This has enabled them to work long hours, travel extensively or relocate without regard to family commitments. The ideal employee was, and to a large extent still is, someone who works full-time and continuously (without breaks for childcare) and never allows family demands to interfere with work. Until relatively recently, it was unthinkable for a man to ask for leave for family reasons, for example, to care for a sick child, unless perhaps he was a widower. Even now, it is considered much less reasonable for a man to ask for concessions for family reasons, and those men who do take time for family activities tend to do so covertly.[1] In general, they keep quiet about the need to balance work with family responsibilities, because to do otherwise would result in their job commitment and ambition being questioned. There is still a prevalent view that job commitment can only be demonstrated by what are often unnecessarily long hours, where an employee is seen to be working. Long hours do not equate with higher productivity and are often counterproductive. However, this expectation persists and causes considerable pressure, particularly for employed parents with young children.

Employed women, especially those working in what were previously considered male-dominated occupations, are generally expected to work in and conform to a workplace designed for men with full-time backup at home.[2] Working women have their own needs. They may need time for childcare. They may need to develop their careers at a different pace or time than men without childcare responsibilities. Does this mean that they are deviant or difficult employees? This is only true if single-earner men with homemaker wives are regarded as the norm, and such a view is increasingly out of touch with reality. Both men and women nowadays need greater flexibility than that offered by traditional patterns of work. Managers who cling to the notion of the ideal employee as someone who does not need to spend time with his or her family, are out of touch with the needs of most employed men and women. Organisations which constrain employees' family involvement are likely to find their policies counterproductive. A growing number of senior managers are themselves members of dual-earner families, and they have a central role to play in changing management styles and organisational policies.

WHY THE WORKPLACE HAS TO CHANGE

If companies are to respond to the changing needs of the workforce, managers need an understanding of the issues faced by dual-earner families and others with family responsibilities. It is important to recognise the practical difficulties that dual-earner partners are likely to face, as well as the contributions they can make and the wider implications for organisational change. Our research examined the problems and rewards of dual-earner lifestyles and assessed the levels and causes of stress among dual-earner spouses. The potential for stress for those working in traditional organisations is just one of many reasons why organisations must change, and why the traditional, male work ethic must be challenged.

Stress

Our research shows that dual-earner men and women who work in unresponsive, inflexible organisations are more dissatisfied with their jobs and suffer higher levels of stress than those in organisations which respond to their needs for a healthy balance between work and family.[3] They are often overloaded by the demands of work and family, or suffer conflict between the demands of each, especially if they have young children or elderly or sick relatives. This can cause poor motivation and productivity, ill-health and high turnover. A study of highly successful and healthy executives of both sexes in the USA demonstrated that these are not workaholics, catching only occasional glimpses of their families. Rather, they are people who have achieved a healthy balance in their lives, with a satisfying level of involvement in both family and work.[4] Responding to the need of dual-earner employees is important for the health of the workforce. This involves the questioning of basic assumptions about gender, careers and the nature of work.

Demographic changes

The fall in the birth rate and subsequent shortage of school leavers in the 1990s means that organisations can no longer rely on the traditional recruitment pool of young, white males. Of course, women have always been recruited into the workforce, but the majority are still employed in low-paid jobs with few opportunities for advancement, often under-utilising their abilities in order to find part-time or flexible work to fit in with their family responsibilities. Organisations which continue to utilise women chiefly as cheap labour or in undemanding jobs fail to recruit and promote from the widest pool of talent. Retention of trained staff will also become difficult in organisations which do not allow sufficient flexibility for all employees with family responsibilities. The recession has taken away the immediacy of this argument in the short term, but companies that take a long-term view recognise the need to develop all their employees, and to ensure a sufficient number of skilled people when the economy recovers.

Britain in Europe

In terms of public policy to facilitate the balancing of work and family, Britain lags behind the rest of Europe. Elsewhere, the public provision of childcare facilities is much greater than that available in the UK (it could hardly be less) and maternity leave provisions are generally superior to those in this country. Most European countries, including those in Eastern Europe, have some system of paid paternity leave and paid leave to care for a sick child, neither of which are, at present, available as statutory rights in the UK. Many European countries also provide for parental leave, that is, a system whereby either parent is entitled to a period of leave for childcare after the end of maternity leave, often with some pay, and with guaranteed reinstatement in their job on the return to work.

Europe has had considerable impact on equal opportunity legislation in Britain in the past, and the more progressive European work/family policies may, in time, create change in public policy on work and the family in this country. Meanwhile, employees with young families may be attracted to leave Britain to work elsewhere in Europe, but are unlikely to move from other European states to Britain with its inferior resources for employed parents. Lack of government intervention places more responsibility on organisations in the public and private sectors to provide the facilities which are provided by governments elsewhere. Organisations which implement childcare and family-leave policies may be able to recruit more widely and may, indeed, be anticipating legislative changes. Implementing these policies voluntarily, rather than waiting for legislation, will provide them with a competitive edge in terms of recruitment and retention.

Equal opportunities
Most organisations have an equal opportunities policy and many also have equal opportunities officers to ensure optimum policies and practices. For 'equality of opportunity' to be a reality, however, it is important to go beyond making provisions for women, such as part-time work or career breaks, while at the same time expecting men who are committed to their careers to work full time and continuously. Provisions to facilitate the balancing of work and family are always available to men in principle, but the perceived cost to men of using these provisions is usually formidable. An understanding of issues faced by dual-earner men and women demonstrates the importance of questioning basic organisational and managerial values, and working out ways of enabling both men and women to make an optimum contribution to the organisation as well as within the family.

It makes good business sense
Until recently, equal opportunity arguments have tended to focus on the ethical and social values rather than the many commercial benefits of a balanced workforce. The business-led campaign, *Opportunity 2000*, which encourages companies to work towards more equal representation of men and women at all levels, is based on a strong business case. The campaign points to companies such as Digital and Xerox, where equal opportunities have resulted in improved communication, effective teamwork, increased productivity, and ultimately, higher profits.[5] Researchers at Ashridge Management Centre have identified a number of sound commercial explanations for the link between equal opportunities and organisational effectiveness.[6] These include:

- **Development of all the workforce**. Companies which enable employees to combine career and family life, and remove artificial barriers to promotion will secure a good return on human resources investment. High-calibre employees will choose to work for, and be committed to, these organisations.
- **Getting close to clients or customers**. Management needs to be sensitive to the major issues affecting their customers. A balanced workforce, with men and women (and representatives of different ethnic and other groups) at all levels, is better able to respond to customer or client needs.
- **The value of differences**. Heterogeneous teams are more creative and innovative than homogeneous ones. The management of diverse groups also requires specific skills. The

enhanced development of managers, which results from managing diversity, enables them to be more flexible and better able to respond to change.

The issues facing dual-earner families demonstrate that for equality of opportunities to begin to become a reality, it is necessary not only to consider family oriented policies, but also to radically rethink what has long been taken for granted about the ideal employee and the ideal career pattern. Many organisations are now taking steps to enable women with families to manage their careers. The focus on dual-earner families demonstrates that this is not just a women's issue. A non-stressed, healthy and effective workforce depends on management styles and policies which allow men and women to lead balanced, productive and rewarding lives and recognises that work and family are important, and indeed, interdependent for both sexes.

In the remainder of this book we explore issues facing dual-earner families and the organisations in which they are employed. This is based on a programme of research involving over 400 dual-earner spouses. The majority were employed in professional, managerial or clerical occupations, with a small number in blue-collar jobs. They included parents of young children, childless couples and couples expecting their first child. We consider the implications for management of the changes in employees' lifestyles and needs identified by our research, and suggest some possible solutions to dilemmas which threaten to hold back the careers and reduce the potential organisational contribution of men and women, including some of the most talented and highly trained members of the workforce.

REFERENCES

1. Hall, D T (1990) 'Promoting work/family balance: An organizational change approach', *American Psychologist*.
2. Cook, A (1992) 'Can work requirements change to accommodate the needs of dual-earner families?' in S Lewis, D Izraeli and H Hootsmans (eds) *Dual-Earner Families: International Perspectives*, Sage, London.
3. Lewis, S and Cooper, C L (1987) 'Stress in dual earner couples and stage in the life cycle', *Journal of Occupational Psychology*, 60, 289–303.
4. Quick, J C, Nelson, D J and Quick, J D (1990) *Stress and*

Challenge at the Top: The Paradox of the Healthy Executive, Wiley, Chichester.

5. Hammond, V and Holton, V (1991) *A Balanced Workforce. Achieving Cultural Change For Women: A Comparative Study*, Ashridge Management Research Group.

6. Hammond, V and Holton (1991) ibid.

2
Stress and Coping at Work

OCCUPATIONAL STRESS AND THE MALE MODEL OF WORK

Although careers can be major sources of life satisfaction, occupations can also be sources of stress. Occupational stress may be manifested in a range of symptoms, including physical illness, psychological distress and low productivity. The causes of stress at work are usually described primarily in terms of job demands, but they are not restricted to the work environment. It is increasingly apparent that the demands of the home, and particularly the problem of juggling family and work, are also significantly related to occupational stress. This is particularly true of members of dual-earner families. A demanding career may involve long hours of work, and the additional demands of domestic life and childcare can cause people to feel overloaded. There may also be conflict between the demands of career and family roles, as work schedules are often incompatible with family life.

In order to examine sources and consequences of stress, we surveyed 310 dual-earner spouses, in a range of occupations. Most of the respondents reported some feelings of overload and conflict, although the majority were coping well and avoiding major symptoms of stress. Although the dual-career lifestyle is very demanding, it is not necessarily stressful. Indeed, multiple demands can be very satisfying if they are well managed.

> I have the satisfaction of knowing I have reached the heights of my career and not missed out on family life and motherhood. (Company Executive, female)

Nevertheless, some dual-career spouses in our study did report symptoms of stress, and most felt that the demands made upon them could be reduced. An examination of the major causes of stress for both childless couples and parents of young children, revealed that these pressures are usually the consequence, either directly or indirectly, of traditional gender stereotypes and expectations. These attitudes underlie the male model of work described in Chapter 1 . In the past, men were able to subordinate the demands of all other aspects of their lives to their work, because of women's willingness to subordinate their own careers to those of their husbands. Traditional men with homemaker wives could sustain intense work involvement, and this has created a norm to which contemporary men and women are expected to conform. It can present problems for members of egalitarian dual-earner families, particularly if they have, or intend to have, children.

Need for a 'wife' at home

Men outnumber women, dominating the higher echelons of professional and managerial worlds. Most have achieved success with the support of a wife who is either a full-time housewife or who has continued to fulfil major domestic tasks in addition to labour force participation. This pattern continues even among some dual-career couples:

> Michael works long hours. He'd rather work doing what he's qualified to do and pay someone else to do menial tasks. He's happy to take the baby for a walk but he won't change nappies or cook a meal. I spend more time with the children, and do the work at weekends, as we have no living-in help. I accept that his career has priority. (Personnel Officer, female)

This level of support enables an ambitious husband (or less frequently, an ambitious wife) to maintain a single-minded level of work involvement, to work long hours, to travel away from home and to relocate when necessary. During the stage when careers are being developed, the workaholic lifestyle may leave little time for life outside work, and even in single breadwinner families this can cause considerable family strain.[1] A wife who caters for everyday needs enables a man to work at a relentless pace and perform at his peak. Women must compete on these terms. Frequently they lament that they, too, need a wife, particularly if they are working in competitive, male-dominated occupations. A female sales manager explained:

> I'm in what is basically a male-oriented world. It is unusual for a woman to be in the sales field and I can see why. Most of my colleagues have got wives or girlfriends to go home to.

They fulfil this other function of fitting in the daily chores which need to be done in order to be up and starting at base point again the next day. For us it's different; we tend to be running to catch up with ourselves before we've got up, so to speak. I think that's true of most people who have jobs where the expectation is that someone else is available to take on the pressure of organising one's life.

Many occupations are so demanding that they can be considered a 'two-person career',[2] which implies that the back-up support of a spouse is essential. Spouses, usually wives, may provide services such as editing or clerical assistance, directly substituting for the work of a paid employee, and assist with entertaining and socialising, which can enhance a spouse's position in the organisation. These services are additional to the provision of emotional and domestic support. Many companies recognise that a wife is an asset, though they often fail to recognise that she may have her own career. The husband of the career wife is often perceived as a liability:

The company believes that men should have wives and that they are an advantage. If you move around a lot, the wife can be looking after the children and buying a new house while he is at work. I don't have a wife to do that for me, which makes life a bit difficult. (Trainee Manager, female)

When I go for interviews, it is assumed that my having a wife is a sign of maturity and stability, whereas I think a woman with a husband and family is thought to show signs of being tied down and inflexible. (Engineer, male)

With the demise of the male breadwinner family, men as well as women find the traditional male work orientation difficult to accommodate with family life. There may be company pressure on men to conform to stereotypical roles and to ensure that family commitments do not encroach upon work. Often, however, the pressures are self-imposed, due to the internalisation of the male work-orientation and the need to conform and compete on an equal basis with single earners. A trademark agent explained the problem as he perceived it:

In our job we have targets to meet and you can't say to the man who works in the office next door that my target should be less than his, because he has a wife at home and I haven't. It's just unfair on him. You are imposing different performance standards which you can't, well I think you can't, justify.

Competing in a male dominated world therefore, means that dual-earner women and men must often conform to the example set by men pursuing 'two-person careers' with the support of full-time helpmates.

In the remainder of this chapter, we consider some of the work-related sources of stress experienced by dual-earner spouses as a consequence of the male model of work, and examine some of the strategies used to cope with these pressures.

WORK OVERLOAD: LONG HOURS AND THE WORKAHOLIC SYNDROME

When someone feels that their workload is so great that they are constantly under pressure, they can be said to be suffering from work overload. A civil servant and mother of a young baby illustrates this problem:

> I feel I've constantly got more things to do than I have time for. It's partly because I work for a head of department who is very good, but very ambitious, and pushes everyone else. It's hard work keeping up with her. I just feel under constant pressure the whole time.

For members of dual-earner partnerships, overload is usually a consequence of intense demands both at work and at home. In this section we examine occupational demands in terms of hours at work and the potential for overload at work. In reality, however, work overload cannot be considered in isolation from family demands, as the two are interdependent.

In our survey, work overload emerged as a very significant source of stress for dual-earner couples, whether or not they had children. The habit of putting in long hours at work tends to be established early in a person's career, and is often perceived initially as an investment for the future. Indeed, long hours at the workplace, perhaps combined with additional studying, may be regarded as a necessary early foundation for career success.

> My hours, according to the time clock in the office, work out at about 48 to 50 hours a week and then I do another 18 hours at home, because I am studying for an extra degree. Ann probably works from about 8.30 to nine-ish in the morning

until about 5 or 6 and then three nights a week, on average, when she has calls to make in the evenings and will arrive home anytime between 8 and 10. Both of us are at the stage in our careers when you have to put these hours in to climb up the ladder. The hours will diminish, hopefully, after four or five years. (Lawyer, male, no children)

Once the pattern of devoting long hours to work has been established, it often becomes a permanent way of life. In many cases, this is because the work and the associated pressure and successes are experienced as rewarding and satisfying. It is possible to become addicted to this way of life. This is the beginning of the workaholic syndrome. A lawyer, who with his spouse had decided that they would not have children, explained:

I really enjoy the work I do so it doesn't matter if it spills over to the weekend. Maybe I'll get sick of it after 10 or 20 years. But I think it's true to say that I enjoy stress anyway, so I enjoy the long hours. I'm quite masochistic, I suppose. I know many of my colleagues see it more in terms of something you have to go through. It's a penance for the next few years. But I thrive on it.

Other people agree that working at a relentless pace becomes a way of life, but are less enthusiastic about it. A chartered accountant explained why she believed that substantial overtime becomes the norm in certain occupations:

I think that once people have qualified, perhaps having done all that studying gets them into the frame of mind of working long hours. They get used to it and also it cuts them off from a lot of interests and a lot of friends they had before. They used to study on top of a full day's work and then they tend to fill up this time with overtime and that becomes accepted as the norm. I don't think it's just in accountancy. I've seen it with friends in other professions, too.

Long hours of work, which replace time spent in studying or which are seen as an investment for the future by ambitious young people, create an expectation that people will be able to sustain patterns of work which later may be difficult to reconcile with family life. The problem is that attempts to modify hours of work for family reasons may then be seen by management as an indication of reduced commitment and ambition, and may be regarded by colleagues as professional suicide. A male sales manager maintained:

> I have published office hours of 8.45 to 5.15, but nobody in my position can just work those kind of hours and survive in a competitive world.

Excess time given to work is time unavailable for family activities, for childcare, for domestic work and for family leisure activities. In single-earner couples, excessive work hours by the breadwinner often mean that the spouse has to raise the children virtually as a 'single parent'. For dual-earners, long hours of work by both partners may leave little time for their relationship, while long hours spent at work by one partner usually increases the family work of the spouse and can cause resentment. Several dual-career spouses referred to problems created by their own and their partners' long hours of work, in terms of relationship or family disruption:

> I left my last job because of the hours, really. I had to work late most evenings. When I got home the children were asleep, and I just never had any time with my husband except late in the evening, when I was exhausted. I think the relationship would have broken up if I had continued. (Catering Manager, female)

SCHEDULE INCOMPATIBILITY AND INFLEXIBILITY

It is not only the number of hours worked which is potentially stressful for dual-earner couples, but also the extent to which each partner's schedules fit in with those of their spouse and with other family needs. Incompatibility of work and home schedules is mainly a problem affecting the parents of young children, for whom it can be a source of considerable conflict. Rigid schedules of work can also create difficulties in dealing with unforeseen circumstances. Even for childless couples, there may be difficulty fitting in health-care appointments or other daytime commitments. Inflexible schedules of work have been associated not only with work-family conflict, but also with reduced job and life satisfaction and poor mental health.[3] Long or inconvenient hours of work are much less stressful if there is a degree of flexibility and control. Flexibility allows spouses, especially parents, to put in the necessary amount of time at work and to do so during hours that fit in with other demands, enabling them to collect children from school or to take time off when necessary, and make up the hours when it is convenient.

In order to assess the extent of work/family management problems, we asked dual-earner spouses, with and without children, to indicate how easy or difficult it was to adapt their work schedules for family reasons. We also asked how satisfied they were with the flexibility of their job. The responses varied to some extent with different occupations but, not surprisingly, it was clear that parents of young children experienced many more problems than childless couples in fitting in work and family demands. However, the vast majority of both parents and non-parents, while accepting that certain aspects of their jobs, by their very nature, were not flexible, believed that it would be possible and desirable to have a greater level of flexibility and control over some aspects of their work schedules.

'Lack of flexibility' in their jobs was a particularly significant pressure for fathers. In attempting to modify work schedules for personal reasons, childless men are not violating gender expectations, but if they do so because of involvement in childcare, this tends to be viewed negatively. Conflict between the demands of professional and parental schedules occurs for both sexes, although it is usually greater for women.[4] However, our respondents felt that employers are often more tolerant of work/family conflicts in women than in men. A man who takes time off work to care for a sick child, or who restricts his hours at work to accommodate childcare, is generally viewed as a less committed employee than one who does not allow family to impinge upon work.[5] It is often assumed that family participation (by men and by women) is associated with decreased commitment and performance at work, but this ignores the fact that many people are highly committed to both domains. Inability to attend to family needs because of inflexible schedules can have a negative impact on productivity and efficiency and can be counterproductive, as this woman lecturer in a college of further education commented:

> OK, so I'm there, I do not take time off because my child's ill. My contribution under stress, having to be physically there and worried about her, may be less valuable than if I had taken the time off and worked from home and made up the time later.

SPILLOVER

Another source of pressure for dual-career spouses is spillover from work to family. Spillover occurs in three different forms: spillover of work itself into family time; spillover of work attitudes into family interactions; and spillover of job satisfaction or stress to life outside work.

Spillover of work into family time

Commitments beyond normal working hours include the need to bring work home, to attend meetings and conferences, to travel extensively, or even to go out in the evenings with colleagues. Such commitments are usually considered important from a career perspective, but if they occur frequently they can interfere with family life, causing conflict of loyalties. The wife of an executive who travelled regularly complained:

> It is very difficult when he works weekends. Being away a couple of nights in the week doesn't bother anybody. It's part of the job and we expect it. It's just fortunate I don't have to travel with my job, so that I'm here for the children. But it does affect our family life when he is away at weekends. That's when we could all be together as a family and relax a bit together.

Although overtime or bringing work home may impinge upon family time, it need not be stressful for the individual. People who can choose to work overtime when it is convenient are in control and, therefore, experience less work/family conflict[6] than those who have no choice. So control over hours of working is important for feelings of well-being.

Spillover of behaviour and attitudes from work to family

In traditional families, where work and family roles are segregated on the basis of gender, behaviours appropriate to each domain can be cultivated. The combining of work and family roles in dual-career spouses means that appropriate behaviours must to be displayed in each domain by both partners; confident and assertive behaviour at work, nurturant behaviour at home. Sandra Bem[7] described the tendency to combine certain stereotypical masculine and feminine traits, so as to react appropriately in a range of situations, as *androgyny*. Androgynous individuals tend to enjoy better mental health than stereotypical masculine or feminine individuals who are unable to be, for instance, dominant or caring in the appropriate context.

Many occupations , particularly those which have traditionally been male-dominated, require individuals of both sexes to be competitive, assertive and achievement-oriented – although the value of more feminine characteristics in the workplace and especially in management styles are beginning to be acknowledged.[8] Dual-earner spouses who combine professional and family work have to switch from the style of behaviour deemed appropriate at work to non-competitive behaviours at home. Inevitably, there are occasions when the switch cannot easily be made; when work attitudes and behaviours spill over to family interactions. A college lecturer complained of her sales manager husband:

> If I tell him about some success I've had at work, he immediately responds with something good he's done. I know he's used to competing all the time at work so that it just becomes a habit to try to outdo everybody else. But it's not what I want. I want him to share my successes, to praise me occasionally, not to feel that we are in competition.

It seems likely that the husband of this woman is displaying what is known as Type A behaviour.[9] Type A individuals are competitive, hostile, extremely involved in their work, impatient and very time-urgent. Unlike more relaxed Type Bs, Type A individuals try to achieve more and more in less and less time and compete relentlessly with themselves and others. Type A individuals create a great deal of stress for themselves and may be vulnerable to stress-related illnesses, particularly coronary heart disease.[10] As Type A behaviour tends to be elicited by a specific situation, usually a competitive work environment, it may be possible to be Type A at work and more relaxed at home. Nevertheless, a study of male administrators[11] found that the wives of Type A men reported much lower marital satisfaction than the wives of Type B men, which suggests that this behaviour does spill over into family life. Many organisations encourage the Type A behaviour pattern, by an emphasis on competitiveness, tight deadlines and intense work involvement, but it is important to recognise that Type A behaviour can create family disharmony as well as increasing vulnerability to life-threatening, stress-related illness.

Spillover of stress and satisfaction

There has been much debate about whether or not satisfaction or stress from work does spill over into family life and vice versa. An alternative view is that the two areas compensate for each other. The notion of compensation implies that satisfaction at work compensates for dissatisfaction at home and vice versa.

This means that an individual with a difficult marital relationship may put more effort into gaining satisfaction at work, and someone who is stressed at work will try harder to gain their satisfactions from their home life. While the idea of compensation seems plausible, the majority of research supports the notion of spillover.[12] This implies that stress or satisfaction at work will have an impact on life outside work and relationships at home will affect experiences at work. Spillover can thus occur in either direction and may be positive or negative.

We found several examples of stress at work spilling over into family life. Stressed individuals are often aware of taking out their frustrations on their family, but are unable to prevent themselves from doing so:

> When I have a particularly bad day at work, I know I'm horrible to live with. I shout at the kids and take it out on my husband. I'm tense and bad-tempered and it affects everyone, although I still manage to be nice to everyone at work. (Personnel Officer, female)

The stress experienced by one spouse is often experienced by their partner, too.

HOW DO PEOPLE COPE?

During a series of interviews with dual-earner partners we asked them how they coped with the pressures of their lifestyle. A number of coping strategies emerged.

Questioning the need for long hours and the workaholic syndrome

Several of the participants in our study questioned whether long hours and workaholism are really productive:

> The workaholic syndrome flourishes here. It is assumed that everybody who wants to get on will be prepared to put the organisation first at all times. Its no good for marriages and I'm not convinced that its really good for productivity and efficiency in the long term. (Journalist, male)

> Most of the people I work with don't seem to value their time off. There's an awful lot of people who don't take their full holiday allocation and who work an awful lot of overtime. They seem almost obsessed with work and that's difficult, because that becomes accepted as the norm. Really, this

often goes beyond the point of reason, because they work overtime to the point where they must become fairly inefficient. When you are working until 1.00 in the morning and then coming back on the job at 7 in the morning, well, to me the work I would have done between 10pm and 1am, I could have done in half the time the next morning. (Chartered Accountant, female)

Choosing part-time work

Reducing the number of hours worked to part-time, especially during the years of early childrearing, can be one solution to work and family overload, but many people find this unacceptable because of the associated loss of benefits:

You lose out on course development and promotion if you are part-time. You are not taken seriously. I'd like to have a part-time job in terms of having more time, but it would be a disaster career-wise. I want to be taken seriously, not left out when decisions are taken, which is what happens to part-time staff. I've witnessed the decline of colleagues who have changed to part-time. (Midwife Tutor, female)

I am committed to my profession and I want to be taken seriously, but I don't want to be working all hours. I want some time with my children. I wish it were possible to work part-time without losing my foot on the ladder. (Lecturer, father of two)

Coping with heavy workloads – managing time

A heavy workload can be less stressful if effective techniques of time management are utilised. Most of the couples we interviewed had found ways of managing their time, which enabled them, with varying degrees of success, to reduce their workload or to cope with short term overload. Strategies used included:

Being assertive
Being assertive involves being clear about one's goals and priorities. It also involves being able to say 'No' to demands which may cause overload (see chapter 7 for a fuller discussion of assertiveness). A lecturer who felt that she had, after much soul-searching, reached a point at which she could now say 'no' explained:

I'm managing my time a lot better now. I'm saying no to

people and I'm not giving them things when they want them if I can't manage it. I'm much clearer now about responsibilities and recognising that I have some personal home responsibilities, as well as work responsibilities.

Similarly, a chartered accountant explained how she had made life easier my stating explicitly what she was and was not willing to do in terms of overtime:

To a certain extent I know I'm putting myself on the line, but I have stated that I'm only prepared to do a reasonable amount of overtime. When I think it is unreasonable, I'll say I'm not doing it.

Fear of 'putting themselves on the line' may prevent over-burdened employees from taking such actions.

Establishing priorities and dealing with temporary situations
Often periods of excessive workload are inevitable and it is necessary to find ways of coping with these for a short duration. A chartered accountant described the problems of studying for exams, in addition to full-time work, while her daughter was a baby. In the face of enormous demands and potential conflicts, she and her husband organised their time in a way they found effective and satisfying.

The way we worked it was that I worked during the week and did all my studying during the week too, so we could have the weekends free. I think most students work two or possibly three evenings, have a couple of evenings off and plan to work on Sunday. I never did that. It was the week-ends when I had time for the baby. Dave did all the cooking and put Amy to bed in the week, but I had the whole weekend free with her.

By being clear about this time plan, she was able to work without any feelings of guilt during the week, knowing that her week-ends would be totally free. Equally, she did not feel guilty about not studying at weekends because of the clear allocation of time.

Although the period of raising young children may be of a longer duration than the period of study for professional exam-inations, it can also be regarded as a temporary situation in the perspective of a lifetime career.

Managing time as a couple

Some couples approached time management as a couple rather

than as two separate individuals, recognising their interdependence by developing joint strategies:

> We tried to reconcile work and home by agreeing a timetable whereby I try to work early in the mornings. Mark does the breakfasts and I go to work at 7.30 am and then I'm home in time for when the nanny leaves in the evening and he can stay late if he needs to.

This appears to be a well thought out, workable and equitable solution. Interestingly, however, this woman felt that she had not completely escaped the impact of gendered expectations.

> It's a way of coping and it works. But I was aware in suggesting it that I got the raw deal, because the kids are tired and grumpy in the evenings and putting them to bed is a struggle, while getting them up isn't. So I still think there's something about, as a woman, taking on the difficult bits, the nastiest bits.

Attempting to manage time as a couple frequently raises issues about responsibility, gender and 'the woman's lot'. Adjustments made to working hours to help balance the demands of two jobs and families are more usually made by the woman, while adjustments made by men are more likely to involve a reduction in time allocated to the family.[13] Insofar as this is in keeping with stereotypical roles, the pattern may be slow to change. Nevertheless, there is a growing minority of couples where time management strategies favour the wife's career. This usually occurs when the wife's occupation involves less flexible hours than that of the husband, but it also requires an acceptance of non-traditional roles. The director of a small firm described his approach to the management of time, which was clearly organised around his wife's career and the demands of childcare:

> Its just a question of making the best use of time. I can't do anything before 10 or after 4. That doesn't bother me because it enables Margaret to hold down a secure and satisfying job and I make enough money to live on comfortably. I've got my work organised optimally during the hours available.

Coping with spillover

The strategies used by our interviewees for coping with spillover ranged from creating clear boundaries between work and home, to taking more drastic steps, such as making a career change. It has been suggested that men tend to experience dual roles sequentially, while women experience them simultaneously.[14] This suggests that women will have more difficulty than men in creating clear boundaries between work and home, because they carry with them thoughts about family much of the time. Preventing family from impinging on work is, therefore, more difficult for many women. Some people make a conscious effort to compartmentalise their lives, so as to ensure that work attitudes and stress do not impinge on their life outside work.

> Once I close the office door, that is it. I switch off completely and start to think about the children, the evening meal and so forth. I would never take work home. (Solicitor, female)

In drawing boundaries, women in particular often experience conflict about areas related to professional development. Society tolerates ambitions in women, but expects a less professional commitment in mothers. This means that some women have to assertively stand up for the right to continue to build their careers after they have children. One way in which our respondents resolved conflict about additional commitments, such as attending conferences, was to involve other family members. Others took care to explain and negotiate with other family members. It is easier to explain commitments to a spouse than to children, but even quite young children can understand a situation which is clearly communicated to them. This can reduce guilt, particularly for mothers whose work spills into family time. One mother who sometimes finds it necessary to work at home in the evenings and during weekends, and who has two young daughters, said:

> It works because Mark is able to support me and play with them and he makes it understandable to them. We worked together to make it alright for them. I don't feel guilty.

It is much more difficult to cope with work stress and dissatisfaction which spill over to create tension at home. Setting boundaries works in some cases, but it is difficult to switch off feelings of anxiety, depression, or dissatisfaction which are symptoms of stress at work. Sometimes it is necessary to take action to provide the space and time to get things into perspective. One respondent described how a period of study, away from her job, enabled her to recognise the stress she had been suffering, which in her case led to a decision to make a career change.

Intellectually, I can do all the job analysis and stress analysis stuff and recognise it in that sense. But it was only by being away from this environment that I actually experienced the change. Being a student I had no responsibility, no pressure. I could manage without working evenings and weekends. Above all, the practical elements of the course gave me the chance to do something I enjoyed and could do well. I suppose what it did was to give me some confidence back, in that there was no recognition for competence in my job. I suddenly found that I could enjoy life. I certainly became an easier person to live with. I was no longer grumpy and bad-tempered with Ben and the girls all the time. I enjoy my work and I'm a nicer person at home.

It is necessary to recognise work stress and the effect of spillover on family life before steps can be taken to change the situation. A period of 'time out' can be instrumental in enabling individuals to recognise the stress they are experiencing, and to see how their life both at home and at work might be different

HOW CAN ORGANISATIONS HELP?

There are a number of implications for organisational practice:

1. The traditional organisation, which functions with the male breadwinner and homemaker wife as its model family, creates the potential for overload and conflict for dual-earner spouses attempting to fulfill multiple demands. Stress audits can be carried out to investigate the prevalence of stress-related symptoms and the causes of pressure and attempts can be made to reduce prevalent stressors. Although many stressors arise solely from work, the significance of the interface beetween work and family as a potential source of stress should not be overlooked.

2. The workaholic syndrome, and the Type A behaviour pattern which is often associated with it, are both counterproductive. Such extreme work involvement and stress-producing behaviours are often associated with ill health and with relationship problems. However, the organisational climate of many workplaces encourages these behaviours. Managers need to recognise Type A behaviour in themselves and others, and to endeavour to discourage employees from adopting these behavioural styles. Examination of their own behaviours is important to ensure that they are not role

models for stress-inducing behaviour. Too often, organisations do not question the value of workaholic behaviour until a key management figure suffers a heart attack.

3. Workloads are less likely to become stressful if employees have some control and autonomy over number and flexibility of hours worked, and are able to modify work schedules without damaging career prospects. Chapter 7 considers alternative work strategies for increasing flexibility and control for those with family commitments. For real autonomy to exist, there has to be an atmosphere of trust, such that managers are confident that employees not working in the conventional time and place are nevertheless working conscientiously and efficiently. Autonomy breeds responsible attitudes to work to a much greater extent than autocratic systems.

4. Work spilling over into family time can create stress and family friction. Many dual-earner spouses fear that refusing to put in extra hours of work would be career limiting. It is important to delineate clear boundaries between work and family time and managers can again serve as role models by demonstrating their own unwillingness to impinge on family time.

5. The stressors identified in this chapter, and the coping strategies adopted by those who are successfully managing work and family, point to the need for training programmes in such skills as time management, assertiveness and stress management. These are discussed further in Chapter 8.

REFERENCES

1. Seidenberg, R (1973) *Corporate Wives, Corporate Casualties*, AMACOM, New York.

2. Papenak, H (1973) 'Men, Women and Work: Reflections on the two person career', *American Journal of Sociology*, 78, 852–872.

3. Pleck, J H and Staines, G L (1983) 'Work schedules and work family conflict in two earner couples', in J Aldous (ed) *Two Paychecks: Life in Dual Earner Couples*, Sage, Beverly Hills, California.

4. Lewis, S and Cooper, C L (1987) 'Stress in dual earner couples and stage in the life cycle', *Journal of Occupational Psychology*, 60, 289–303.
   Also, Sekaran, U (1985) 'The paths to mental health: An

exploratory study of husbands and wives in dual career families', *Journal of Occupational Psychology*, 58, 2, 129–138.
5. Lamb, M E, Russell, G and Sagi, A (1983) *Fatherhood and Family Policy*, Lawrence Erlbaum Associates, Hillsdale, New Jersey.
6. Pleck, J H and Staines, G L (1983) op cit.
7. Bem, S (1974) 'The measurement of psychological androgyny', *Journal of Consulting and Clinical Psychology*, 42, 2, 153–162.
8. Davidson, M and Cooper, C L (1992) *Shattering the Glass Ceiling: The Woman Manager*, Paul Chapman Publishers, London.
9. Friedman, M and Rosenman, R H (1974) *Type A Behaviour and Your Heart*, Knopf, New York.
10. Booth-Kewley, S and Friedman, M (1987) 'Psychological predictors of heart disease: A quantitative review', *Psychological Bulletin*, 101, 343–362.
11. Burke, R J, Weir, T and Dulvors, R E (1979) 'Type A behaviour of administrators and wives' reports of marital satisfaction', *Journal of Applied Psychology*, 59, 9–14.
12. Zedeck, S and Mosier, K L (1990) 'Work in the family and employing organizations', *American Psychologist*, 45, 240–251.
13. Kingston, P W and Nock, S L (1985) 'Consequences of the family work day', *Journal of Marriage and the Family*, 47, 620–629.
14. Hall, D T (1971) 'A model of coping with role conflict: The role behaviour of college educated women', *Administrative Science Quarterly*, 1, 7, 471–486.

3

Issues in Career Development

This chapter focuses on dual-career partners in professional and managerial fields.

PREPARING FOR A DUAL-CAREER RELATIONSHIP

Professional and executive careers typically require a high level of commitment and training. Individuals are encouraged to plan their careers by setting intermediate and long-term goals, and working out the best way to progress from one stage to the next. This is not always straightforward, as career planning and progress often depend on unpredictable circumstances. However, if career planning is difficult for individuals, it is even more complex for members of dual career couples who have to organise and plan their future, to take account of both partners' aspirations and to enable them to integrate work and family life. Careers officers, teachers and others may offer considerable advice on the choice and planning of a career, but the planning for future family life and the integration of work and family receive less attention.

Couples planning a dual-career marriage need to discuss with each other their aspirations in career terms, and also the implications of these aims for their relationship and for their family life. Are both careers considered to be equally important, or will one career be given priority, either throughout the marriage or only at certain points in time? The implications of these decisions for choice of where to live and decisions about mobility also need to be discussed. What will happen if one partner is required to relocate with his or her job? Partners also need to talk through such issues as *how* domestic work is to be shared, whether or not they want children and, if so, how they would cope with the extra demands of parenting.

If issues concerning career commitment and family are not discussed initially, problems may subsequently arise when partners discover that they have conflicting expectations from the marriage. Uma Sekaran, who has extensively researched dual-career family issues in the USA, quotes a young divorced career woman who felt that she and her former husband had been so taken up with each other before their marriage that they had talked only vaguely about their future. She had believed she would have no problem in handling both career and marriage. Too late, she realised her husband expected her to be at home when he returned from work, to have a meal ready, and also that he was anxious to start a family immediately, regardless of her career aspirations. Inevitably, the marriage failed.[1] If such issues are explored before marriage, compromises may be reached or a couple may realise that their ambitions are incompatible before a commitment is made. Often there will be an agreement on basic attitudes, so that at this stage it is merely a question of working out the implications. Initial agreement on basic issues does not guarantee that one partner will not change later, but an awareness of the problems involved in combining two careers and a family does allow for some form of preparation.

Making plans, being flexible

Several of the couples we interviewed were aware of the possible pitfalls and had developed highly detailed plans. For the majority, an agreement on basic values was considered to be sufficient. As one male sales manager suggested:

> I would say we didn't take any conscious decisions on Day One. It just evolved, but I don't think we'd have done it any other way. There were certainly no clearcut plans, with dates set in concrete. But we did agree on basic philosophy from the outset and that is very important. Of course, we argue about isolated incidents, but as long as we agree on the basics we can discuss problems and work things out.

Most couples emphasise the importance of flexibility and the ability to adapt plans, as it is impossible to predict every possible contingency. If one or both partners do not find jobs where and when they had planned or achieve their desired promotions, they usually have to compromise on such matters as commuting, increasing travelling time or delaying starting a family. This is why agreement on basic principles is considered by most couples to be more helpful than the establishment of detailed, intricately worked out plans. This is highlighted by a male dentist of a dual-career couple:

The key has been planning and organisation and sometimes manipulating the system. Of course, the plans haven't always worked out, so we had to adapt them; perhaps when a job didn't come up in the right place and at the right time. Once I had to do an enormous amount of travelling, so that Helen could continue her training. Being flexible and willing to adapt is important too.

Establishing attitudes to division of labour

One of the most important basic principles which couples feel should be established concerns attitudes to gender roles. On a practical level, establishing norms of who does what and who is responsible for what is important in order to avoid conflicts and misunderstandings at a later stage, as emphasised by this female systems analyst:

> I would not do a lot different myself except for the old adage of start as you mean to go on. It's difficult to go back later. I often used to think, 'Blow it, I'll do it myself,' because I didn't like to bother him. Now if I have to ask him to do something it's considered an extra, whereas if we'd started off that way, it would be taken for granted.

It may be helpful in this context to 'talk through' attitudes to gender expectations, as partners may feel guilty or uneasy about not conforming to stereotypes, as this female paediatrician illustrates:

> I still have the feeling that it's me who should be home for the children in the holidays, or me who should be going to school events. I don't think mothers ever find it easy to get away from these feelings of guilt.

Issues of equality and the implications for mobility also need to be considered. Many women find their aspirations blocked by lack of mobility because of their partner's career, and men are frequently expected to be free to relocate without regard to their wives' careers. The possibility of future transfers should be anticipated and the question of how they would be handled discussed, so that problems can be dealt with more easily if and when they do arise.

The shortage of role models for a non-traditional, dual-career lifestyle may create difficulties, so it is imperative that these issues are considered in advance. Research indicates that the daughters of employed mothers, whatever their occupational status, have less traditional gender attitudes and are more likely to plan for sustained career involvement and an egalitarian marriage.[2] Employed mothers may often provide a model of the successful integration of work and family roles, especially when this is accompanied by increased paternal involvement in the family. Men and women from more traditional backgrounds may be committed to an egalitarian partnership, but often have more difficulty in discarding the outmoded patterns of behaviour which they have observed in their parents.

Choice of location

One of the first decisions to be made by dual-career couples is where they will live; this is usually determined by where they work. When both partners work in the same area there is no problem, but if they are both working or are offered jobs in different parts of the country, the decision about where to live becomes more difficult. With traditional couples this situation causes no dilemma as it is accepted that, even though the wife may be working, the husband's career should take precedence. When both careers are equally important, however, there is no tried and tested formula for dealing with the question of where to live. For some, it is possible to choose a location which is equidistant from both jobs, even though considerable travelling may be involved. For other couples, jobs are too far apart to allow commuting from one home. It then becomes necessary to work out a solution which will take account of the needs and aspirations of both partners.

Looking for jobs in the same location

When couples are entering the job market at the same time, both partners, at least initially, will seek work in the same location. Job seeking can be difficult, even for individual applicants, especially in times of high unemployment, but it is much more difficult for couples. Dual-career couples need to find two jobs, both of which will allow them to satisfy their own career needs and provide prospects for advancement. Their jobs should enable them to live together and co-ordinate their schedules, to give them some free time together and, if necessary, to fit in childcare. The task of seeking jobs which fit these needs is daunting.

There are a number of job-seeking strategies which can be adopted by dual-career couples:

- The husband locates a job first and the wife follows him. This is the traditional strategy.
- The wife locates a job first and her husband then seeks work in the same area. This is non-traditional.

Neither of these strategies can be considered egalitarian, although they may work well in specific circumstances. A number of more egalitarian strategies can be adopted.

- Each spouse looks for a job independently, and the couple choose the best joint option.
- Spouses may apply as a unit either to the same employer or in the same geographical area.
- Spouses may apply for one job, that is, to job share (see Chapter 6).
- Each partner may accept the best opportunity available in any location, and then live apart during the week.

A study of the job-seeking strategies of over 400 young scientists in dual-career marriages revealed that, whilst most initial job-seeking strategies and some final decisions were egalitarian, the majority of final decisions were traditional, that is, the husband accepted a job first and the wife followed.[3] This was the case even with people who professed to hold feminist attitudes.[4] Why should professional couples who start out with a commitment to the ideals of equality usually resort to following traditional patterns? Most couples in this study said they would have preferred a non-traditional decision if the options had been available, but they were unable to do so because of job constraints. Many felt that time was running out and only one partner had been offered a job. Frequently, the husband's job was given priority because it tended to be more highly paid, and this swung the balance in his favour.

The impact of gender role stereotypes on job-seeking and the choice of location

One reason why men are more likely to find a job, and a more highly paid or desirable situation than their partners, is prejudice and, often, active discrimination against married women. Many employers regard married women as unreliable employees, because they view them as potential mothers and because they believe that women will sacrifice their own jobs to move with their husbands' careers. Unfortunately, this belief tends to become self-fulfilling. Given an employment market in which married women are discriminated against and married men secure the best jobs, women whose own ambitions are frustrated may become more willing to move with their husbands. The problem of discrimination against married women is illustrated by two general practitioners, who had been looking for partnerships at the same time.

> We were both looking at the same time, but in practice we had to wait for Robin to get a job first. There were no problems with hospital jobs, because they were all short-term contracts and there were never any questions at interviews about family and children and that sort of thing. But when we started looking for permanent partnerships, that was the first thing they asked me at interviews. Anyone who was thinking of taking me on would be thinking of taking me on for many years and they thought that if Robin didn't have a job, I would end up moving with him. So, although in theory we were applying for jobs at the same time, it was a bit of a non-starter for me. In the end he found a partnership and I took a part-time post, which was all I could get in the same area. (Doctor, female)

Creative solutions, which would maximise the satisfactions of both partners, were blocked by constraints in the labour market and by practical considerations. The husband of the GP quoted above explained that:

> We tried various options. We even applied to job-share, just one full-time job between us. Most people didn't even bother to reply. You just apply to advertisements in the *BMJ* and there's very little information about the person to whom you are applying. One or two wrote back and said that was a very interesting idea, but not suitable. The only other option would have been to apply to a single family practice, but there are lots of problems with that. It's difficult to have holidays together, you have to get people in while you are away. And it means that if you are on call, you share it between you, whereas if you are in different practices, as we are now, we try to be both on call the same weekend. It messes up one weekend, but it frees the other.

Occasionally, because a wife finds a job first, a decision is made to live near her job and for the husband to look for work in the same geographical area. This is often experienced as a stressful alternative, because deferring to the wife's career conflicts with the traditional stereotype of what is acceptable male behaviour. Michael Berger and his associates quote an example of one couple who had adopted this strategy.[5] The wife had taken up a job and her husband had followed, but was unable to secure a position. Although both partners were content with the decision, they nevertheless felt it was necessary to conceal the fact of the husband's unemployment from their parents. Indeed, they went to great lengths to pretend he was employed. This even involved the husband taking the parents to his wife's office and pretending it was his own. Another problem is that men who follow their wives and look for a position in a restricted geographical area are often regarded by prospective employers as being less committed to their profession than those who put their own career first.

Stress and satisfaction in joint job-seeking

The process of simultaneous job-seeking for dual-career couples can be stressful. Spouses often find that they have to deal with issues of competition and power because, unless two suitable positions are readily available, one partner may have to accept a position at the expense of the other. This may lead to a sense of failure if they are unable to live up to their egalitarian ideals. The converse of this is that there is considerable satisfaction to be gained from joint job-seeking, especially when problems are worked out. Partners often feel that they have proved themselves ready to make sacrifices in the interest of equality, and this may strengthen the relationship.

Choice of locations when both partners are already established in jobs

Couples who already have jobs at the beginning of their relationship may face similar problems. Highly educated, career-orientated women tend to delay marriage until they are established in their careers. To some extent, this avoids the problems of discrimination described by married women seeking jobs at the same time as their spouse. However, problems arise when both partners have established careers in different geographical areas. Strategies used to deal with this dilemma include compromise, alternating the location in favour of each spouse, and commuting.

Problem solving and compromise

Although it is often necessary to give priority to one spouse's career, a decision can be reached by considering all aspects of the problem and reaching a compromise on the basis of logical decision-making, rather than because of gender stereotypes (although the decision frequently upholds such stereotypes). A consultant physician explained that:

> My husband got his consultancy first, so we moved and I transferred to a position here. He was offered posts in nicer places, but chose to be in a large city so there would be more opportunities for me. Also, to be fair, there are fewer posts available in his speciality than mine and that had to be considered, too.

It is possible that reports of such a logical approach are simply rationalisations to justify decisions after they have been made. Nevertheless, it does appear that many couples are now considering all aspects of such a situation, giving equal weight to the needs of each career.

Alternating decisions in favour of each partner
When decisions about location are made in favour of one partner, it is often with a recognition that, if the occasion arises, decisions about further moves will favour the other spouse. Often this decision takes account of the fact that one partner may wish to take a break for childrearing at some stage. A lecturer in business studies explains the dilemma she and her partner faced and the solution they reached:

> We were unusual, I think, because I would have said that normally one goes to where one's husband's livelihood is. He was working and living in Scotland and I was running a business here at the time and I didn't go there. He gave up his job and found one with a firm here. That was my condition, but of course it suited him too. We knew the decision may be different later.

Later in the marriage, her husband was relocated. By then they had a young baby and the mother took a career break and moved with her husband. Dilemmas were thus resolved as they arose by alternating decisions in favour of each partner and taking account of circumstances at the time.

Commuter marriages – living apart together

For some couples, it is not possible to reach an acceptable solution which enables them to fulfil both partners' career needs and to live together. Even if a compromise or a wholly satisfactory arrangement is reached, this does not guarantee that the problem will not recur. Many spouses, particularly wives who were satisfied with their original location decision, later feel constrained.

> We came here at first because I was working here, so Michael found a job here, too. Then he accepted a partnership in the firm of solicitors he was with and, of course, that is relatively permanent. Then I was very restricted. It would have been much easier to have progressed in my career if I could have looked for jobs elsewhere. I suppose I didn't consider working in a different town at that time. I have thought about it recently but now we have children it seems really impossible. I do feel frustrated because I have missed out on opportunities. (Systems Analyst)

> My only problem is that if I want promotion I have to go to London and my husband has said that there is no way he will give up his job and go back to London. I think this is a major problem facing many couples. (Manager)

These dilemmas illustrate once again the need to be flexible and to continually reappraise situations. Plans and compromises made early in marriage may become unsatisfactory or unworkable at a later stage. One solution to this dilemma is for couples to live apart either during the week or for longer periods.

Naomi Gerstel and Harriet Gross interviewed 50 couples who spent at least three nights a week in separate residences, although married and intending to remain so.[6] Separation was due to participation in careers which involved different locations. They concluded that the success or otherwise of this arrangement depended upon a number of factors:

- *Age.* Commuter marriages work better for older couples who have had time to cement their marriages.
- *Children.* The problems of increased childcare responsibility for one partner complicate this arrangement for parents. Commuting is easier for couples who have no children or whose children have already left home.
- *Distance.* A relatively short distance between locations, enabling partners to see each other regularly, is less stressful than distances which force long separations.
- *Conditions of employment.* Flexibility of working hours and the use of computers and other equipment for working from

home can reduce the length of time partners need to spend apart. Work that does not spill over into weekends is also important, so that partners can spend their time together without pressures from work impinging upon them.

- *Income.* A high income is essential to maintain two homes, and this can also reduce strain by allowing frequent travel and telephone calls.
- *Lack of permanence of the arrangement.* Most commuting couples see the arrangement as temporary, although this is not necessarily realistic. Defining the situation in this way helps people to cope with separations.
- *Positive attitudes.* Couples who take pride in being able to commute to advance each other's careers, and who reaffirm the importance of being married, are the most likely to find living apart a satisfactory experience.

Living apart can threaten the sense of what marriage should be, and diminish each partner's sense of security. Individuals may feel depressed, lonely or resentful about each other's independence. Often a period of adjustment is necessary when partners do have time together. On the positive side, it can increase the romantic attachment of husbands and wives, equalise the division of labour and open new horizons for career advancement. Overall, however, Gerstel and Gross conclude that it is a forced choice, the benefits of which will outweigh the costs only in specific situations. Furthermore, they add, these costs are never entirely absent.[7] It is never an easy option, but one which may sometimes be preferable to the alternatives.

> When my husband moved to his new job, I stayed on for the girls to finish school. I think that was the loneliest, most unhappy period of my life. The trouble was that I was too proud to admit it. Sometimes I would tell him not to worry about coming home at a weekend if he was very busy, but if he took me up on it I was devastated.

PARENTING, CAREERS AND MOBILITY

Perhaps the most difficult decisions facing dual-career couples, and those intricately linked to career mobility and relocation issues, are about whether or not to have children and, if so, how to plan the timing of childbearing and childrearing to fit in with their careers. Often there is pressure from relatives or friends to conform to the prevalent view of a 'real' family by having children. Occasionally, there is also conflict between husband and wife on this issue:

> My parents and my husband think I should have a family by now. I have to choose between a career and children, it seems, or try to do both jobs inadequately. I haven't decided what to do yet. (Senior Technician, female)

Although the decision to have a child is normally taken by both spouses, most recognise that the implications tend to be greater for the woman. A manager who elected not to have children commented:

> I think it is the case for a lot of women that they have to make the choice between career success and family, and what really rankles me is that men simply don't have to make that choice. I feel they don't, because they put the burden on women.

Women no longer expect to cease employment on marriage, as they often did in earlier generations, but the majority do take their first break from employment when their first child is born. Many also subsequently reduce their career involvement because of the difficulty in balancing career and childcare. It is still widely believed that mothers should assume the major responsibility for children, and this can create feelings of guilt in women who continue to pursue their careers whilst their children are young. Mothers are expected to put family before career, but fathers are not expected to allow family to interfere with their work. This often means that even when fathers are eager to participate equally in childcare, the demands of their jobs prevent them from so doing. Lack of adequate childcare provisions, together with long and inflexible hours of work, often make it difficult for both parents to work full-time. It is usually the mother who accommodates her career to care for children.

Not surprisingly, fears of not being able to manage both motherhood and career, and anxieties about the constraints which motherhood will place upon career advancement, feature prominently in decisions and conflicts about whether or not to start a family.

> I would like to have a baby, but I don't know how I would manage. I'd like to work part-time, but that isn't possible with this firm. I might find someone else to jobshare with, but otherwise it just wouldn't work. (Personnel Manager)

Mothers who do return to their career after childbirth often confront prejudiced attitudes in employers.

There is a lot of prejudice about women with young children in this organisation. I'm really frightened that if I have a child, it will ruin my chances of promotion. It's so unfair, nobody ever takes account of a man's family. (Systems Analyst)

Thus, dual-career couples often face considerable conflict. There may be pressure to start a family and conform with the predominant view of the 'average' married couple. Traditional attitudes to the roles of mothers and fathers often make this a difficult decision.

Delaying decisions about parenting

Improvements in contraception and obstetrics mean that women can now choose to delay the birth of a first child. Since the 1960s, there has been a rise in the average age at which women marry and a trend to delay first births. A common pattern in earlier decades was for women to enter or re-enter the labour force after their children were of school age. Whilst many professional women continue to follow this pattern, there is a realisation among career-oriented women that there are disadvantages in doing this. Interruptions for childbirth have little impact on traditional female occupations such as clerical work, but they do tend to limit access to occupations with more of a career structure:

If you are trying to get back into the profession at the age of 40, there isn't much chance. This is the problem, the child-bearing years are the same years when you have to build your career. For a woman who drops out for a period of, say, five to ten years, it would be difficult to get back. You would be out of touch anyway. (Chartered Accountant, female)

Couples who delay parenthood until they are well established in their careers usually have greater flexibility in managing competing demands. They are also more likely to be able to afford quality childcare. Many couples feel that waiting until the time is right is the ideal strategy.

We both spent time working in hospitals and then we travelled a bit. Then we both found partnerships and spent a year moving into a new home. The time seemed right and we decided to have a baby. (Doctor, male)

> We will wait until we can afford to have somebody to look after them, a nanny that is, before we think about children. I don't think there will be any problem if we can afford proper help. (Radiologist, male)

Where career advancement is assured, it is rational to delay having children. However, a crisis point occurs for many women in their thirties. At this stage they are often beginning to establish themselves in their career, but at the same time there is an awareness that time is running out for childbearing. Career-related dilemmas about whether to start a family were described as a major source of stress in a recent survey of women managers.[8]

Delaying parenthood is often a temporary strategy in the face of a difficult decision. Some parents maintain they never made an actual decision:

> I think it's one of those things where you keep thinking I'll have children in a couple of years, but then by accident I became pregnant, so then you are faced with a *fait accompli.* (Chartered Accountant)

Other couples who put off having children until the time is right realise at some stage that it is too late. Studies of 'intentionally' childfree women suggest that many expected that as a matter of course they would have children, but eventually realised that they had made implicit decisions to remain childfree.[9]

Voluntary childlessness

The deliberate decision not to have children is still unusual, although the number of voluntarily childless couples is increasing. A study of 'intentionally' childless wives in Britain indicated that, like women who delay parenting, they tend to be well-educated, often career-oriented, and married to men in professional or managerial occupations. Thus, although voluntary childlessness remains a minority decision, it is more common among dual-career couples.

Couples who decide not to have children take into consideration their own personal needs, career issues and social expectations. Social norms which encourage childbearing can make the decision more difficult. In spite of this, a growing minority of women and men are questioning the inevitability of parenthood. For some the decision is very easy:

> The decision not to have children was never difficult for me.

I just don't like babies. I never wanted all the hassle. If I could have given birth to a couple of teenagers, that would have been great. Adrian knew this before we married. I was sterilised and have not regretted it. (University Lecturer)

It must be said that most people find this decision more difficult. There is usually some conflict between the desire to have children and career ambitions. Voluntary childlessness is a choice made when the career-related costs of parenthood seem too high, particularly for women who also fear the loss of independence.

I took a conscious decision years ago not to have children, because I was concerned about becoming dependent on somebody else's income, being constrained and not being able to seek my way in the world, in the way that men can. (Insurance Agent, female).

It has been argued that women's choice of childlessness may be interpreted as a protest against the heavy burdens which parenthood places on mothers.[10] Many women report that in an ideal society they would like to have children, but that given current attitudes to mothers, lack of childcare provisions and the unresponsiveness of employers to parents, they decide to avoid what they regard as an untenable situation rather than attempting to modify it. This decision frees them from the burden of combining career and family, but ironically it does not always guarantee an escape from prejudiced attitudes. Some employers regard all women of childbearing age as potential mothers, and women who make known their decision not to have children are often regarded as deviant.

You can't win really. The bosses think women with children are unreliable and lack ambition, but both male and female colleagues are suspicious of me because I don't intend to have kids. (Public Relations Officer, female)

'Intentionally' childfree couples tend to minimise the stress of appearing different from the 'normal' family by restricting their social network to people in a similar situation.

There's no peer group pressure. Of our circle of friends only one couple have children so it's not as if we are meeting people at weekends with children all over the place. Also the people living here in these flats are all either career couples without children or single people. (Lawyer, male)

Establishing clear priorities – planning for children

If a couple decide that they do want children, the next decision to be made concerns the timing of pregnancy so as to take account of the career demands of both partners, especially the mother. Some couples regard children as a priority and careers are fitted around the family, rather than the other way around. This does not inevitably involve sacrificing professional opportunities.

> I had my children at various points during my training and career. The oldest was born whilst I was at medical school and the youngest after I became a consultant. You see, children are very important to me. I wanted a career too, but I didn't want to give up the chance of having a family. A lot of married women doctors delay having children. They pick the best posts, which might mean living separately from their husbands for much of the time. Then they wait to become a consultant. Often they will have difficulty being appointed, because employers are suspicious of married women with no children. They think they will be going off on maternity leave as soon as they are appointed. And all the time these women's fertility is declining. I didn't know if I'd make it to become a consultant, so I had my family when it was convenient and I made it anyway. (Consultant Paediatrician with four children)

This woman was able to combine her two roles successfully, largely because of a scheme for part-time training in the National Health Service for doctors and dentists with domestic commitments. For those in other occupations, especially where supply exceeds demand and there is fierce competition, this may not be so easy.

THE STRESS OF JOB MOBILITY AND RELOCATION

Decisions about job mobility and relocation can be particularly difficult for dual-career families. The problem of relocating can be considerable, even for single earners who have to take account of factors such as children's education and social networks. Added to this, career needs of the spouse can cause particular problems in dual-career couples.

Relocating decisions, like decisions concerning initial locations, tend overwhelmingly to be in the traditional vein – in other words, to favour the husband's career. As Lucia Gilbert put it in her book on men in dual-career families:

> That location and relocation decisions tend to reflect traditional attitudes is not surprising, although this does not necessarily mitigate the stress of these decisions, nor the constraints on those who decide not to move. Women and men currently choosing a dual-career family lifestyle live in a largely patriarchal society; they are subjected to and influenced by the norms and values of this society as well as its structures.[11]

It is more socially acceptable for a wife to follow her husband than vice versa, and wives are more likely to feel that they should put their family's needs before their own. In addition, the practicalities of the situation often favour husbands, as men are more frequently offered higher status posts or higher salaries than their wives. For women in dual-career families, relocations can cause considerable frustration. A study of women managers in the UK found that the majority of those who were able to accept relocation were unmarried.[12] Just under a quarter of all women managers interviewed were not mobile because of their partners' careers or because of other commitments.

The decision for men to refuse to relocate is non-traditional. Although women frequently accept constraints on mobility for family reasons, men have begun to do so only relatively recently. Consequently, there is still an expectation that men will be mobile (and that women will not be mobile, which can affect promotional decisions). Men who do not conform to this expectation are often regarded as lacking in professional commitment and their promotional opportunities may also be restricted. The constraints are nevertheless acceptable to men who value their participation in family life and accept the importance of their spouse's career. An engineer who accepted limited mobility, because his wife was a doctor in general practice, felt that there were sufficient opportunities for him within his geographical area. However, his involvement in childcare imposed further restrictions on him which he felt prospective employers had difficulty in understanding:

> I went for an interview recently and in the first few minutes after we sat down, the interviewer went over the three most important points. One was that I should be completely mobile; be free to work in London or Paris for a few weeks. I

said no, I thought I had made it clear in my application form
that I have a wife who is in practice here and I have a young
child. I suppose they just assumed that my wife would take
over.

Decisions by men or women to refuse jobs which require mobility
or to resist relocation are by no means always easy. Even for
couples who have considered the question in advance, making
the actual decision can be very stressful, and for those who have
to confront an unexpected situation, it can perpetuate a crisis:

> When the organisation I used to work for closed its Northern
> branch, I was offered a position in London. The alternative
> was redundancy. It was difficult because Carolyn had a
> secure position with the local authority here and, in fact, she
> earned more than I did. We talked about it a lot and con-
> sidered the pros and cons. She didn't want to move and
> didn't think she could find an equivalent position elsewhere
> so easily. The stress of the decision-making caused us to
> argue a great deal and say a lot of acrimonious things we
> both regretted. Eventually, we decided to stay put. I was
> unemployed for nearly a year. I felt resentful, and I know she
> felt guilty. Somehow we survived and I found another
> position. (Computer Programmer, male)

The situation which this man described was stressful, not only
because the refusal to locate resulted in a period of unemployment, but also because the decision had favoured his wife's
career. It is not uncommon for wives to follow their husbands in
their job, and then to have periods of unemployment before
finding a position themselves. However, couples who relocate on
the basis of the wife's career often experience problems, because
their behaviour contradicts assumptions of gender-appropriate
behaviour.

A solution which many couples are seeking, and a few organisations are offering, is to relocate as a couple. This might
involve both partners applying for new jobs together in a given
area, or one partner agreeing to relocate on the condition that the
organisation finds a suitable post, with no deterioration in promotion prospects, for his or her partner. This type of policy
requires an enlightened and understanding attitude on the part
of the employer, and may also involve considerable negotiation,
planning and problem-solving on the part of the couple themselves. The tortuous processes involved in achieving such a

solution are illustrated by the experiences of Kathy and Richard. The impetus for the move came from Kathy:

> The college approached me about a year ago to ask if I would be interested in setting up a new department. They offered me a very attractive package which included the opportunity to work part of the time in the community, a car, a higher salary and relocation expenses. They also found a position for Richard. That was part of the package. Richard did not want to go, though. He's not as ambitious as me and he said he was happy in his present job. We talked about it for months and at one stage I was going to turn the job down. After all, what's the use of an interesting job if it ruins my marriage? My personal life is important, too. Eventually the college wrote to Richard, stressing that they really valued his experience, and wanted him in his own right. After all, he is an expert in his field. After that he decided to go. There were some difficult times before we actually reached a decision that we would both move. (Lecturer, female)

It appeared that Richard feared that he was being appointed as an incentive for his wife to move, rather than being valued in his own right. This fear was echoed by other spouses who were considering relocating as part of a couple. A female academic, younger and less professionally advanced than her spouse, voiced this opinion:

> There were two posts available at the same university and we did think that we might both apply. I wasn't entirely happy about the idea because we would have presented ourselves as a package; we both come, or not at all. John already has his PhD and a lot more publications than I have, and I was afraid they might offer me a job in order to attract him and I wouldn't have been considered on my own merit.

As more men and women refuse to relocate, or agree to do so only as part of a package involving their spouse, organisations may eventually be forced to recognise the realities of the dual-career lifestyle and take steps to make relocating decisions easier. However, it is likely that individuals committed to both career and family may continue for some time to be faced with dilemmas and tough decisions. There are ways, however, in which the dual-career couple may be encouraged to plan for the problems confronting this 'new workforce'.

HOW CAN ORGANISATIONS HELP?

1. Dual-career partners can be encouraged to incorporate family decisions in career planning by, for example, career counselling and appraisal systems which acknowledge the legitimacy of non-traditional career paths.
2. Recruitment and selection procedures can be adapted to meet the needs of dual-earner partners involved in joint job seeking (see Chapter 9).
3. Companies can modify their relocation policies and practice in a number of ways:
   — First, for those individuals (and families) who need to be moved, organisations should provide the support required. This means help with buying and selling houses, helping spouses find equivalent jobs, and allowing the individual and the family enough opportunities to familiarise themselves with the new location.
   — Second, organisations could consider gearing their relocation plans to an individual's 'home life' phases. It is obviously the case that at certain phases of a dual-career family cycle, change is less disruptive than at other phases (children beginning school, spouse re-entering career). On occasions, moving a person may be inevitable and necessary (e.g. when an engineer possesses skills vital to a particular project), but in most cases any planned change could be considered in light of the individual and family circumstances, with a view to integrating them into the changes and demands of work.
   — Third, the spouse's role in the individual's job and career development has been almost ignored by employing organisations. It would seem reasonable that the spouse should be given 'the option' to get involved in the decision-making and information-sharing process concerning any move that may impinge on the family. At the moment, organisations are contracting with one element of the family unit, but making decisions which radically affect the unit as a whole. By operating in this way they often cause conflict between the individual and his/her family.
   — Fourth, it is frequently the case that organisations provide their employee with inadequate notice regarding geographic moves. This usually involves them in a

period of separation from their family, which may adversely affect them, their family, and in the long run the company, which may suffer from less efficient work performance as a direct consequence of the domestic conflicts.

— Fifth, the major sources of stress involved in any potential move stem from the uncertainty which is nurtured in organisations by misleading or often imprecise information about their career plans given to employees. Up-to-date, honest communications can only help to minimise the level of uncertainty about prospective developments and provide for greater acceptance and a smoother transition when it occurs.

— Sixth, the organisation will have to reconsider its attitudes toward women executives. It will have to offer promotional moves to them on the same basis as male managers and will also have to provide women (and men) with the opportunities to refuse a transfer without damaging their promotional prospects or with the same support facilities as given to their male counterparts if they accept (e.g. helping to find the husband a job, temporary 'home help', relocation expenses, paying the differential on mortgage rates, etc.). Implications for relocation are discussed further in Chapter 9.

This is a time of great social changes, and corporate planners will need to be insightful, creative and innovative in designing effective strategies to deal with them.

REFERENCES

1. Sekaran, U (1986). *Dual Career Families*, Jossey-Bass, San Francisco.
2. Keith, P H (1981). 'Sex-role attitudes, family plans and career orientations: Implications for counselling', *The Vocational Guidance Quarterly*, 29, 244–252.
3. Berger, M, Foster, M A and Wallston, B S (1978) 'I will follow him: myth, reality or forced choice? Job seeking experiences of dual career couples', *Psychology of Women Quarterly*, 3, 9–21.
4. Foster, M A, Wallston, B S and Berger, H (1980). 'Feminist orientation and job seeking behaviour among dual career couples', *Sex Roles*, 6, 7, 59–67.

5. Berger, M, Foster, M A and Wallston, B S (1978) op cit.
6. Gerstel, N and Gross, H (1984) *Commuter Marriage: A Study of Work and Family*, Guilford Press, New York.
7. Ibid.
8. Davidson, M and Cooper, C L (1983) *Stress and the Woman Manager*, Blackwells, Oxford.
9. Veevers, J E (1982) 'Researching voluntary childlessness: a critical assessment of current strategies and findings', in Macklin, E and Rubin, R (eds), *Contemporary Families and Alternative Lifestyles*, Sage, Beverly Hills, California.
10. Bram, S (1978) 'Through the looking glass: voluntary childlessness as a mirror of parenthood', in Miller, W B and Newman, L F *The First Child and Family Formation*, Carolina Population Center, North Carolina.
11. Gilbert, L (1985) *Two Careers/One Family*, Sage, Beverly Hills, California.
12. Davidson, M and Cooper, C L (1983) op cit.

4

Managing Transitions: Parenthood

For those dual-earner couples with children, the transition to parenthood is a major life event which has a significant impact on their career and experience of work. In this chapter, we consider some of the dilemmas that face new, dual-earner parents, and the implications of these for managers.

Throughout the life cycle there are major transitions to be faced: transitions from school to college, starting a new job, moving house, retiring from work and so on. Each of these changes requires us learn new behaviours to fit into new environments, interact with new people and form new relationships. Every change involves some stress, but can also lead to personal growth and development, with opportunities for increased satisfaction if successful adaptation takes place.

In the past, managers have only been concerned with transitions in employees' work lives. To ensure the smooth running of their departments they may take steps to ease the transition, for example, to new information technology systems, or new locations. Some companies go beyond a concern for immediate productivity and offer counselling or training to ease the transition to retirement, or redundancy counselling to ameliorate the transition to unemployment. However, the belief that work and other areas of life, especially family, are separate spheres, has meant that equally important transitions, and the impact these may have on work, have been neglected.

THE TRANSITION TO PARENTHOOD

The transition to parenthood is clearly a major, career-related event in women's lives, with maternity leave marking a rite of passage. The transition to fatherhood tends to be considered less relevant to a man's career, but this also affects needs and behaviours at work. The birth of a baby causes a major upheaval in family life. Couples have to deal with an enormous new responsibility and intense demands on their time. In addition, further pressure is caused by social expectations about the respective roles of mothers and fathers. The number of mothers returning to their original jobs and full-time employment after maternity leave is growing steadily, but they remain a minority in the UK, and often face criticism because of the persistent belief that mothers of young children ought not to go out to work. (In other European countries, and elsewhere, it is taken for granted that mothers will return to work after having a baby).[1]

Professional and managerial women face conflicting pressures. Alongside the view that mothers ought not to be employed, there is the belief that educated women should not waste their opportunities by remaining at home. In the UK, the situation is exacerbated by lack of public childcare provisions and by inadequate maternity and other leave provisions, as well as by the lack of policies which are responsive to the needs of families in many companies. For fathers, there is the expectation that their involvement with work should not be affected by parenthood, which can create difficulties for men who wish to adapt their work schedules to the needs of the family.

As part of our research programme we examined the impact of the transition to parenthood for dual-earner couples. We looked at pressures and symptoms of stress reported by 47 couples on two occasions: before the birth of their first child and, again, after the wife's return to work.[2] All the mothers-to-be planned to return to their jobs. After maternity leave new dual-earner parents, especially mothers, reported feeling increasingly pressurised by the multiple demands on their time. Many reported that they felt tired all the time, and at first they felt less satisfied with their lives in general than they had before the birth, which suggests that this is a fairly stressful time. However, some surprising results emerged. A small group of women decided not to, or were unable to return to their jobs as planned after maternity leave. These women as well as their partners were much more highly stressed and dissatisfied than the dual-earner parents. Whether or not the mother returns to work, the transition to parenthood appears to inherently stressful in the short term, but for mothers who plan to carry on working and for their spouses, returning to employment reduces the strain of new parenthood. There is some evidence that mothers of young children, regardless of their career orientation, enjoy better mental health if they are employed than if they are not.[3] This may be reflected in their husbands' well-being, balancing out the stress of the multiple demands of the dual-earner lifestyle. Many of the couples in our study, especially those for whom childcare was not a problem, indicated that, despite the hectic nature of their lives, the dual-earner lifestyle enabled them to enjoy parenthood. As one mother put it:

> We enjoy the baby more because we are both working. If I were home all day, I would be frustrated. It's nice to have someone to do the hard work. I just come home and play with her. I have the nice part.

So organisational policies which help mothers to get back to work, and enable fathers to play their part in childcare, are important for the well-being and satisfaction of new parents.

The transition is rarely completely smooth, however. Most of the new dual-earner parents in our study identified problems or dilemmas, while a minority who worked in non-supportive organisations faced extreme difficulties.

DILEMMAS AND ISSUES FOR NEW PARENTS

Renegotiating gender roles and relationships

The birth of a first baby is a major turning-point in a marriage, often resulting in a decline in marital satisfaction and a trend towards a more traditional division of labour, even among couples who had previously enjoyed an egalitarian relationship.[4] Couples who attempt to share 'parenting' as well as 'bread-winning' on an equal basis have to construct and negotiate their roles in a social context, where the accepted norm is for the mother to take on the role of main caregiver, while the father merely 'helps'. This belief in the optional nature of the father's contribution to childcare (and the mother's contribution to breadwinning) is reinforced by the availability of maternity , but not paternity or parental, leave, and by organisational expectations that becoming a father should not affect men's work involvement.

During maternity leave, traditional patterns of behaviour along gender lines are often established. These may continue when the mother returns to work. The more time the father is able to spend with the family at this stage, the more likely it is that the couple will be able to negotiate and establish an equitable and satisfying relationship as parents. By contrast, occupational demands which keep the father away from home for prolonged periods before a baby is born, can create conflict and dissatisfaction in the relationship. As there is evidence that marital dissatisfaction affects job satisfaction,[5] this, in turn, can affect morale at work.

Maternity leave – How long?

A second issue for new dual-earner parents concerns the length of statutory maternity leave the mother should take up to the maximum of 40 weeks. This will depend on a number of factors, including the needs of the woman, her health and energy, the couple's personal and financial situation and the circumstances of her job. Some of the women in our study were back at work within a few weeks of the birth, others took their full leave entitlement, and sometimes still experienced practical or emotional difficulties in leaving the baby. There is no ideal length of leave, either from the perspective of mothers or employers, as there is little advantage in mothers returning to work before they are physically or psychologically ready.

We found that the major considerations affecting the length of leave taken were career and financial factors, frustration at home and beliefs about the baby's needs. For some women, dissatisfaction with being at home full-time, or the perceived need to compete with men on equal terms, pulled them back into the workplace at the earliest possible time.

> I tried staying at home for several months with my first baby. I was bored and took it out on the family. I learned my lesson and returned to work three weeks after my second baby was born. (Manager)

> I had two children and took the minimum amount of leave each time. Then I made it very clear to everyone that my family was complete. I think that worked in my favour. It demonstrated my commitment to my career and that they wouldn't have to worry about maternity leave once I became a partner. (Chartered Accountant)

Although an early return to work is often deemed necessary from a career point of view, not all women who do return early believe it is ideal. A medical practitioner who returned to work when her baby was six weeks old said, on reflection, that:

> I wouldn't advise anyone to go back so soon ... the whole thing is completely exhausting.

Some women, despite being highly committed to their job, decided to take the maximum leave so that they could enjoy the time with the baby and be able to resume all their duties on their return. Not all women were able to do this, however.

Financial considerations prevent many women from taking their full period of leave, because income is reduced, and, after 18 weeks, leave is unpaid. Some firms now pay women more than the statutory minimum. For others, though, unless their income is non-essential, which is rare, it is difficult to take a longer period of leave, even though a mother may not feel ready to return:

> I had Frankie after working three years. Unfortunately, my husband didn't earn enough to keep us, so I had to go back fairly soon. I worked up to a week before he was born and went back within six weeks. (Computer Programmer).

A chartered accountant pointed out that, not only was she not being paid by her firm during her absence, but the demands of her profession left her out of pocket:

> My employers do not pay me during maternity leave and obviously six months without pay make things very difficult. It's especially difficult because I need a car for work. Obviously, during this six months I've still got the car to pay for, but there is no income coming in to pay for it with. So, if you like, I'm not just not being paid, but I'm actually losing money.

Economic need often prevents women from negotiating better conditions, such as a period of part-time working or working from home. Many are concerned that if they ask for such concessions they would be told to take the full leave of absence, with all the financial implications:

> I felt that I couldn't ask for preferential treatment just because I had a baby. I think there was a fear of being told that if I couldn't fulfil all my duties I should take full maternity leave and I couldn't afford to be on such low pay. (Training Officer).

As two incomes become increasingly necessary for most families, many women are forced to return to work earlier then they would ideally like, and consequently may find the transition particularly difficult.

Returning to work

New mothers seldom return to work without any initial mis-givings, often reinforced by other people's reactions:

> Other women were horrified and asked me how I could leave such a small baby, as though I didn't love him. I felt very guilty. (Designer)

> At first I used to tell people I was going back because I needed the money. I felt I needed to make excuses. But now I tell the truth. I came back because it's what I wanted to do. (Teacher)

A study of women in the USA found that those most likely to plan to return to full-time employment were highly trained, with high levels of career commitment, non-traditional views of women's role in society, with husbands who supported the decision.[6] Our study found that the main difference between women who fulfilled their plans to return to their jobs and other women was age. Older women were more likely to take up their reinstatement rights. Often, they had deliberately delayed childbearing with their career in mind, and tended to have more responsible jobs with higher incomes than other women which contributed to their decisions to continue working.

This might appear to suggest that personal characteristics, especially career commitment, determine whether or not a new mother goes back to work, and, hence, that there is little an organisation can do to influence the decision. Clearly, this is not true. First, there are practical reasons why some women change their minds about returning, particularly difficulties in finding suitable childcare. Practical solutions in terms of childcare assistance, extended career breaks and flexible working patterns help to retain staff after maternity leave. Many women move to jobs which offer better conditions, such as job-sharing or working from home. Second, management structure and policy can also influence women's attachment to their work, at all levels of the organisation. Research has shown that one major factor which determines whether women return to their jobs after maternity leave is how they perceive opportunities for women in their organisation.

In one study,[7] new mothers, even in unskilled work, tended to return to their jobs if they were encouraged by their supervisors to think in career terms and to apply for promotions, and also if they could see other women progressing within the organisation.

By contrast, those mothers who saw no possibility of career prospects of any kind and who saw only men in the management structure, understandably perceived no long-term impact in taking a break from full-time work, and, as a result, were more likely to change their mind about seeking reinstatement. Women who are frustrated in their career, because of lack of recognition or blocked promotions, may decide that a period of full-time motherhood offers a more satisfying alternative. A scientific officer, who did return to her job, illustrates this ambivalence:

> I love my work, but I didn't miss it while I was on maternity leave ... to be honest, I think I should have been promoted by now. If I was a man, I would have been. If it seems that I'm not going to get anywhere, I might consider giving up.

To ask for concessions or not?

A major issue facing new dual-earner parents is whether or not they should ask for concessions such as shorter or more flexible hours, or less travel. Apart from financial considerations discussed above, career ambitions have to be balanced against family needs, so much depends on how parents believe management will respond to requests. In fact, few fathers in our study were entirely happy about asking for concessions. But this was also true of many mothers who did not feel that they could do so, or preferred not to be treated as special cases. Women who are the first to take maternity leave in their organisation, or at a particular level, are sometimes mindful of the need to dispel prejudices about the supposed unreliability of mothers with young children. Many respond by ensuring that colleagues suffer the least possible inconvenience:

> I think the fact that Rosemary made the minimal conceivable disruption, rather than taking all the leave to which she was entitled, actually reinforced the fact that she was a reliable colleague.

While colleagues may react more favourably to the prospect of other women taking maternity leave as a consequence of this course of action, expectations may be raised which other women are unable to live up to. It is only by making known the needs of dual-earner parents that management awareness of these issues will be raised.Of course, there will always be some men and women who are happy to make no concessions to parenthood. There are many more, however, who would like more flexibility, but do not feel able to ask for this, lest it affects their career. Those who are able to combine work and family in a flexible way and to remain highly competent, are in position to force traditional managers to question the validity of traditional, rigid and often workaholic working patterns:

> I recently interviewed a woman and several men for an executive position. The woman told us directly that she intended to have another child and that she intended to leave the office at 5.15 prompt every day. This raised a problem. She was far and away the best applicant, but we work in an environment where it is rare for anyone to leave the office before 6 or 7. Also, we didn't know how we would cope with anyone in such a key position taking maternity leave. We talked about it and decided it was a weakness on our part if we couldn't accommodate the needs of someone who was such a good candidate. We took her on and have never regretted it. (Company Executive)

Reinstatement problems

Although the vast majority of women in our study experienced no problems over reinstatement, some employers did make it difficult or even impossible for new mothers to return to their jobs. At the extreme, three women were made redundant during maternity leave. Only in one case was this genuinely part of a large number of redundancies. Another, a 30 year-old computer consultant, reported that as soon as she told her boss that she was pregnant he made her life miserable. He made it clear that he did not want her back at work after she had the baby. As soon as she began her leave, he appointed a replacement and when she was ready to return, she was told that she was redundant.

An equally illegal stance was taken by the employer of another woman, but this was even more surprising, as the woman and her boss were both lawyers. She felt bitter about losing her job with a firm for which she had worked for seven years, and although she took independent legal action and received a financial settlement, she did not feel that this compensated for the hurt she had suffered. While these cases are extreme, and illegal, a number of less extreme and more common reinstatement issues were also reported.

Changes in the nature of the job

Approximately one third of the new mothers in our study

reported that their jobs had changed in some way. There was a clear distinction between those who were in control of the situation, negotiating change in their favour, and others on whom changes were imposed. The outcome was rarely satisfactory in the latter group. Many new mothers had been replaced permanently, rather than on a temporary basis during their leave. They were then moved to another, often less interesting or less responsible job when they returned, and felt demoralised.

I felt that I was being shunted from pillar to post and no longer had a really useful role in the organisation. (Biochemist)

The decision to convert a temporary to a permanent replacement is often based on the assumption that a new mother is not likely to return to work. It may even be believed that if she does come back, she will not remain in her post for long, or may be less good at her job. There is a danger of this becoming self-fulfilling. Women who are given less challenging work often become disenchanted and confirm such suspicions by leaving their organisations:

My boss just assumed I would not come back and trained someone new. I have been given a much less interesting job and quite honestly I am bored ... I'm looking for another job now. (Laboratory Technician)

Women who were able to negotiate changes in their jobs usually did so to create greater flexibility. The most popular option was a period of part-time work to ease them back into their jobs and sort out childcare arrangements. Others made compromises in other respects: for instance, a nurse who arranged to do more night duty in order to spend time with her baby during the day, while her husband was at work; and an assistant buyer in a large store who elected to do more paperwork to reduce the amount of travel in her work. For these women, the compromises were considered worthwhile to enable them to sustain their careers and spend time with their children. The key point is that changes which are self-initiated are less stressful, because they imply an element of control.

It is widely assumed that any adjustments to the patterns of work after the birth of a child will be made by the mother. In some cases, changes are made by the father, either because his occupation is more flexible or because he wishes to spend more time with the child. For example, one of the new fathers in our study left his job as a designer because he believed that freelance work would give him the greater flexibility necessary for child-care. His wife continued in her full-time job, while he fitted in freelance assignments around childcare. For this father, as for many mothers, the birth of a child was a catalyst that provided an opportunity to explore a new way of working. Motherhood, and to a lesser extent fatherhood, often acts as an incentive to career change.

Accumulation of work after maternity leave

Other women return to an increased workload.The nature of some jobs is such that it is difficult for a woman to be replaced during her absence. A tax inspector described her predicament:

> The nature of the job is such that work cannot be taken over by a temporary replacement, therefore I had two choices. One was to hand over all my cases to someone else on a permanent basis. The alternative was to keep all my files, so that in principle there would be no development on these cases for three months and the correspondence would just pile up.

She chose the latter course, although in practice she did a con-siderable amount of work during her leave so that the work would not mount up. She found this acceptable because it was her decision. Other women, however, believed that a temporary replacement could, and indeed should, have been appointed in their absence. Returning to a build-up of work, in addition to the demands of parenthood can be stressful and is often unnecessary.

> I had insisted on not being replaced permanently, but did not expect not to be replaced at all. Nobody had done any of my work while I was away, so I had to catch up and keep up with the job and cope with a young baby. (Civil Servant)

Lack of support for new parents

While the couples in our study reported that many managers were willing to provide some practical support and concessions, it appears that others were less sympathetic to the needs of new parents and created considerable extra pressure. This can be illustrated by two examples of unhelpful practice. In both cases, not only did management fail to support and encourage mothers back to work, but they created unnecessary difficulties, insisting that no concessions at all should be made to the parents' needs.

Barbara

Barbara is a VDU operator, employed in a large engineering company. Her husband, Ian, is a manager in another firm. Both work inflexible hours and Ian puts in many hours of overtime. Barbara returned to her job when their baby was six months old, partly, she says, for financial reasons and also because she enjoys her work and the company of her colleagues. Initially, childcare presented a problem. There was no workplace nursery at either company and no public nursery places available. It was decided that the baby would be looked after by Barbara's mother. This was not a very satisfactory arrangement as the grandmother lived a considerable distance away. Barbara took responsibility for transporting the baby to his grandparents' home, getting up at five in the morning to do some housework, taking the baby, and then usually arriving at work on time.

Her supervisor was very insistent that Barbara should not 'take advantage' of the fact that she had a baby by arriving late. She was informed of this in no uncertain terms. No account was taken of her domestic situation and difficulties. Then she arrived five minutes late for work on two occasions in one week, and she was given a warning. She felt that rather than considering ways of helping her, the supervisor was implying that she should not really be working. The assumption that her work performance might suffer if she was occasionally five minutes late can be contrasted with the potential effect of this attitude on her work satisfaction and motivation. A satisfied worker who is occasionally and unavoidably late is likely to be more productive than a punctual and disaffected one.

Sally

Sally is employed in a large department store. John, her partner, is a surveyor. Sally returned to work when her baby was three months old and the couple took it in turns to take their daughter to nursery and to collect her after work. On two occasions when the baby became ill at the nursery, Sally was contacted at work. The nature of John's work made him more difficult to contact. The policy of Sally's firm was that if a member of staff was called away during the day, he or she must have written permission from two levels of management before leaving the premises. This unhelpful and rigid policy ensured that Sally felt uneasy about leaving her daughter if there was the slightest possibility of her being unwell, as she knew how difficult it would be for her to get away if there was an emergency.

In both these cases, it was the mother who bore the brunt of inflexible management policies, which arise from an ethos of suspicion of employees, typified by the cliché 'give them an inch and they'll take a mile', rather than an ethos of trust and a desire to assist staff in balancing their work and family commitments. Many of the fathers in our study also reported extreme difficulties, not only in being able to leave work in an emergency, but also in refusing overtime or otherwise restricting their work schedules in order to fit in childcare.

Much of the stress associated with the transition to parenthood for dual-earner couples originates from social expectations, stereotyped assumptions about parental responsibilities and unhelpful management practices. Nevertheless, some managers and some organisations are leading the way by doing much more than paying lip service to supporting dual-earner families. This is achieved by both informal and formal policies and practices.

INFORMAL POLICIES: AN EXAMPLE OF GOOD PRACTICE

John is a training and development manager in a large company. His wife is a lawyer, with another company and they have two teenaged children. He has always attempted to share parenting, although over the years both he and his wife have sometimes encountered difficulties in balancing their careers with childcare and in negotiating a fair distribution of responsibility. John reported that these difficulties affect the way he regards members of his staff when they become parents. He gave the example of Jane, a training officer who came back to work when her baby was three months old. Bearing in mind his own experiences, he was concerned to minimise her difficulties, so he told her that when she was not actually involved in taking courses there was no need for her to be in the office. She could, he maintained, be working just as effectively from home, where she could be contacted by telephone if necessary. Jane was grateful for this consideration. However, she mostly preferred to work in the office rather than at home. On occasions, however, such as when her baby or the childminder were ill, she did work from home if she was not involved in training. She did not abuse the privilege, but reported that the knowledge that she could be more flexible, if necessary, made her feel more in control. She felt that her work and family responsibilities were manageable.

In this case there was no formal change in the overall organisation, so parents elsewhere in the company may have been relatively disadvantaged. It demonstrates that awareness, and especially personal experience of dual-earner family issues, can change the ethos of a particular department, and hence the experiences of some new parents. However, the existence of men and women with family responsibilities in the management structure does not, in itself, guarantee change. Indeed, we found some examples of parents who had progressed into management without making any personal concessions to the need for childcare, and who expected others to do likewise, often overlooking the less privileged positions of other parents. For instance, a tax inspector who was a mother of two, married to a teacher, and employing a nanny said:

> I am fairly intolerant of women who take time off or who leave early because of their children. It gives other women a bad name.

Parents who manage to achieve success through conforming to the male work ethic, often do so by behaving in a manner which resembles that of the traditional father.[8] Their involvement with their children is fairly restricted. Some parents, both mothers and fathers, are comfortable with this, but for others it is an unacceptable price to pay for career success. Those who do behave like traditional fathers often collude in perpetuating organisational structures and management attitudes which are inimical to family life. For this reason, it is not enough to rely on the goodwill and understanding of individual managers. More formal organisational policies are also needed to ease the transition to parenthood. These are discussed in Chapter 9.

IMPLICATIONS FOR ORGANISATIONS

The advantages of facilitating the transition to parenthood

Becoming parents for the first time is a potentially stressful time for both men and women, but the evidence suggests that both parents find it easier to adapt if the mother is enabled to get back to her job. Practices which make it easier for new mothers to get back to work, and new fathers to have time for involvement in childcare, therefore enhance the well-being of dual-earner employees at this stage of their lives. There are also advantages to employers in terms of maintaining organisational commitment, and retaining and motivating trained staff.

Management attitudes

Good or bad practice in relation to employees' work and family experience stems from basic attitudes towards employees. These attitudes concern not only beliefs about gender roles and the ideal worker, but also fundamental management philosophies and trust or suspicion of workers. Some managers oppose policies to allow employees to be flexible about where or when they work, because they do not trust them not to abuse these 'privileges'. However, trust or lack of it tends to become self-fulfilling.

The importance of perceived control for managing transitions

One of the major reasons why life transitions can be stressful is that they create a new situation in which individuals may feel that they have little or no control. One important factor to bear in mind when helping people through this or other transitions is to aim to provide them with a sense of control. We have seen that new parents adapt best when they are able to initiate the necessary changes in their work patterns, and are most distressed when changes are imposed upon them. The changes parents most often want are those which make their jobs more flexible, enabling them to work out the best way for them to manage work and family.

Opportunities for women

New mothers are more likely to return to their jobs and to be committed to the organisation if they are encouraged to think in career rather than just job terms. This applies to all levels and occupations. Women who are encouraged to plan their careers, have role models of women in the management structure and do not experience discrimination will be most highly motivated and committed to the organisation.

Encouraging alternative career paths

Encouraging women to think in career terms does not necessarily imply that they must adhere to traditional career pathways of full-time continuous work. Women can be encouraged to make long-term career plans which include periods of part-time work or breaks from employment. However, as long as this approach to career planning is considered appropriate for women and not for men, women will be relatively disadvantaged in the organisation. Men will also continue to be disadvantaged in terms of time available for family. For alternative career planning to be a genuine option for men and women, several prevalent assumptions must be questioned. These include the widespread belief that career success must be achieved by a certain age, otherwise the person is a failure. Career planning has to be seen as a flexible and lifelong process, with people progressing at different rates according to family needs, in a planned way, while remaining in control of their own lives. Appraisal interviews would be an appropriate place to look at these issues and make plans in the light of both individual and organisational needs.

Social support

The transition to parenthood is a potentially stressful period for new parents, particularly mothers, who tend to assume greater responsibility for childcare. Adjustment to the transition is easier in the context of social support.[9] A generally supportive attitude from management makes it easier for parents to ask for concessions if necessary, and reduces the stress of uncertainty associated with possible unexpected occurrences, such as illness of the child or of the child's carer.

Training

As many of the problems involved in the transition to parenthood arise from a mismatch between social expectations concerning parenthood and paid work, training can play a vital role in challenging outmoded beliefs and ambivalence and providing alternative attitudes and strategies. Training may be directed at managers and supervisors, who can be encouraged to reflect on dual-earner family issues and to reformulate counter-productive attitudes and policies. Equally, training can be useful for prospective or new parents, enhancing personal effectiveness skills at work and at home. (See Chapter 8.)

Childcare assistance

We list this last, not because it is the least important but because it should be considered in the context of the above considerations. There is no doubt that workplace crèches are invaluable for some parents. We discuss the various childcare options in the next chapter. However, it must be emphasised that the usefulness of such initiatives is constrained according to general management awareness of dual-earner family issues, supportiveness, and opportunities for women. Introducing a nursery without attending to these factors can be just a token gesture. It enables women to work, but not to pursue a career, and does nothing to challenge the male work ethic.

REFERENCES

1. Lewis, S, Izraeli, D N and Hootsmans, H (1992) *Dual Earner Families: International Perspectives*, Sage, London.
2. Lewis, S and Cooper, C L (1988) 'The transition to parenthood in two earner couples', *Psychological Medicine*, 18, 477–486.
3. Brannen, J and Moss, P (1991) *Managing Mothers: Dual Earner Households After Maternity Leave*, Unwin Hyman, London.
4. LaRossa, R and LaRossa, M M (1981) *Transition to Parenthood: How Infants Change Families*, Sage, Beverly Hills, California. Also Elliott, S A, Watson, J P and Brough, D I (1985) 'Transition to parenthood in British couples', *Journal of Reproductive and Infant Psychology*, 22, 295–308.
5. Zedeck, S (1992) 'Exploring the domain of work and family concerns', in Zedeck, S (ed) *Work, Family and Organizations*, Jossey-Bass, San Francisco.
6. Behrman, D L (1980) *Family and/or Career: Plans of First Time Mothers*, UMI Research Press, Ann Arbor, Michigan.
7. Newell, S (1990) *New Mothers and Work*, Paper presented at the British Psychological Society's Occupational Conference, Windermere.
8. Rothman, B R (1989) 'Women as fathers: motherhood and childcare under a modified patriarchy', *Gender and Society*, 3, 1, 89–104.
9. Cutrona, C and Suhr, J (1990) 'The transition to parenthood and the importance of social support', in Fisher, S and

Cooper, C L (eds) *On the Move: The Psychology of Change and Transition*, Wiley, London.

5

Workers Have Families Too

We saw in the previous chapter that couples who continue the dual-earner lifesyle after becoming parents, may be less stressed than those who adopt a traditional, single breadwinner structure. This is not to suggest, however, that managing two careers and the care of children or other family members is easy, particularly in the context of a male work ethic which assumes a 'wife' at home. To a large extent, the difficulties experienced by dual-earner parents are the consequence of their own and other people's beliefs about the roles of mothers and fathers. Equally important are the attitudes of their employing organisations to parental responsibilities, their commitment to encouraging women's careers, and the extent to which they are prepared to take practical steps to accommodate parents' needs. In this chapter, we discuss issues related to childcare and care of the elderly as these affect dual-earner families, and consider initiatives which employers can take to facilitate the combining of caring and work demands.

The couples in our survey described two major problems associated with the combining of careers and parenthood: finding the time and energy to cope with the multiple demands and coping with associated conflict.

TIME AND ENERGY

Balanced against the satisfaction of being able to 'have it all' expressed by most couples, was the problem of finding the time and energy to fit in the care of a young child with the demands of two careers. Exhaustion and feelings of 'not having enough hours in the day' were frequent complaints. Generally, everything was fitted in, but at a cost, and it was usually mothers who paid the greater price:

I've felt tired for so long, its just a part of my life since Alex was born. I had plenty of energy before. Now I just accept being tired. (Nurse, mother of 2 year old son)

I don't have time for me, to do what I want. I'm running around all day doing things for everyone else. I'm tired all the time and there's no time left to do the things I really enjoy. (Manager, mother of 4 year old son)

The demands on time and energy do not always decrease as children grow older. Nappies no longer need to be changed, but children have to be transported to school and to a host of other activities:

I think life is rushed because of the children and all their activities and commitments. I don't think it's because of our careers that we are always rushed. (Solicitor, mother of children aged 13, 10 and 2 years)

The cost of combining two careers with parenthood should not be underestimated. Nevertheless, most parents considered this to be worthwhile, as involvement in both career and family provides two sources of satisfaction. Elizabeth Shore, GP, mother of four and wife of Labour MP Peter Shore summed it up well when she remarked:

Having the family and the job was exhausting, but it had the advantage of being two things which were totally different and rewarding in quite different ways.[1]

CONFLICTING DEMANDS

When people feel torn between the needs of children and the demands of work, the subsequent conflict can be distressing:

If my child is ill and I have an important meeting at work I have to decide which I should do first – take her to the doctors or attend the meeting. I constantly feel torn in two directions. (Lawyer, female)

Because work and family compete for scarce time and energy, dual-earner parents are vulnerable to role conflict. Childless couples may also experience conflict between work and family, for instance, when faced with relocation issues. However, although the childless couples in our study reported some conflict between career and family obligations, this was not a source of stress. For dual-earner parents, on the other hand, conflict was the major cause of stress-related symptoms. Other research also indicates that role conflict diminishes job satisfaction, life satisfaction and mental health for dual-earner parents.[2] Conflict between career and family tends to be greater for mothers than for fathers, but men are not immune. A study of professional and managerial men[3] revealed that conflicts related to their workload or work-related travel interfering with family life were common. However, it was men whose wives were also employed in high status occupations who experienced the greatest level of conflict. The demands for greater family involvement by men in dual-career couples creates the potential for conflict between work and family for fathers as well as mothers.

As we saw in Chapter 2, conflict between work and family is partly a consequence of incompatible schedules. There is also the conflict between what parents are actually doing and what they feel society expects them to do, which often causes confusion about identity, particularly for new mothers. The prevailing definition of a 'good' mother is one who is not employed outside the home. Nancy Russo[4] has described what she calls the 'motherhood mandate', which is a powerful unwritten rule that women should bear children and be 'good' mothers. This does not preclude employment, providing this does not interfere with what society defines as good mothering. Russo argues that this guarantees the existence of conflict between motherhood and employment. Other researchers point to a growing belief that bright, educated women should not become immersed in domesticity.[5] Thus, women are exposed to conflicting cultural directives. It seems that they cannot win. Lucia Gilbert and her associates[6] conclude from a study of professional mothers that most women internalise the motherhood mandate and that, even if they reject this at a conscious level, it can still cause feelings of guilt and anxiety:

> There is conflict. There is constant conflict. Perhaps it is my guilt. I think that is what causes the conflict. I'm sure my son isn't as worried as I am. He takes it all in his stride, but I almost feel that he's compartmentalised into one part of my life, which is something I don't want to happen. (Manager, female)

> I'm constantly worrying about him whilst I'm at work. There's times when he's phoned me from school because the after school activities have been cancelled or someone hasn't turned up to bring him home. I live in fear that arrangements will go wrong. (Training Officer, female)

I think that all working mothers feel guilty about leaving their children. I feel guilty, especially about leaving them during school holidays, or if one of them is ill. Sometimes one of them will say, 'Don't go to work today mummy, stay at home with me' and I feel awful. (Paediatrician, female)

This guilt is frequently made worse by open criticism from other people, which can produce considerable tension:

My biggest problem is my mother. She is very critical of me for working when the children are so young and she makes me feel very guilty about it. My two sisters both gave up work when they had children. Sometimes I have bad dreams about my mother dying and that increases the anxiety and guilt. (Scientific Officer, female)

Even women who reject the traditional female role may compare themselves, and their performance at home as a parent, with full-time mothers. Inevitably, such a comparison appears unfavourable, again fostering guilt and self-doubt:

Sometimes I feel guilty and frustrated when I hear that my friends are doing such marvellous things with their children in the holidays – I feel my kids are missing out. (GP, female)

However committed women are to their job or career, they often feel they should spend more time with their children and conform to the popular view of a 'good mother'. Most mothers maintain that their children are the most important aspect of their lives, as do increasing numbers of dual-career fathers, but at the same time women are also aware that life goes on beyond childrearing:

If it's a choice between my career and my son, then there's no choice at all. He comes first. But I'm also conscious that in ten years' time, he will be probably going away to college and I might have missed the opportunity to make a successful career for myself. (Manager, female)

EFFECTS ON CHILDREN

The guilt expressed by many career mothers stems from a belief that children need exclusive maternal care during their formative years. What is the evidence for this view? During the 1950s John Bowlby, a psychoanalyst, introduced the term 'maternal deprivation'.[7] He argued that separation from the mother can have devastating and longlasting effects on the child's development. Bowlby's studies were based largely on children in institutions, whose total life patterns were disrupted and who were deprived of both mothers and fathers. He greatly underestimated the role of the father. It is clear that children do need to form an attachment with their mother and also with their father. However, the regular absence of parents for a few hours a day while the child is cared for elsewhere, cannot be compared with the situation of children in institutions or in hospitals. As Michael Rutter points out in his book *Maternal Deprivation Reassessed*,[8] maternal deprivation is too broad a term to be applied in a general way to all forms of separation. Nevertheless, Bowlby's work has had an enormous impact on society's attitude towards motherhood. Views on the acceptability of maternal employment have changed over the years, but as recently as 1988, when women in a national survey were asked whether they believed it was right for mothers of pre-school aged children to work, 74 per cent said that they should either not work outside the home, or that they should only do so in cases of financial necessity.[9]

Concern about the possible impact separation might have on children led to a spate of research comparing the adjustment and well-being of children of employed and non-employed mothers. The results were unexpected. In most cases, there were no overall differences between the two groups of children and, indeed, several studies have demonstrated that the effect of maternal employment on children is, if anything, beneficial.[10] There is no evidence that the children of working mothers are emotionally or socially deprived. Children of dual-earner parents benefit from greater paternal involvement and tend to be more independent and competent as a result of forming attachments to a number of people.[11] Reviewing the research, Louis Hoffman[12] argued that children benefit from having a mother who is happy and fulfilled, whether as a full-time housewife or as a career mother. A bored, frustrated mother at home is less beneficial to a child than a stimulating nursery or a committed nanny, combined with the attention of parents in the evenings and at weekends. Children of homemaker mothers tend to have more stereotyped sex role attitudes, and daughters have lower self-esteem and aspirations than those of employed mothers.[13] Evidence that high achieving women and those in non-traditional occupations are more likely to be daughters of employed mothers attests to the value of a non-traditional role model for girls in particular.[14]

A recent study in the USA of adolescent daughters in dual-career, dual-earner and single-earner families[15] demonstrated that the extent to which the girls held non-stereotyped views of men's and women's roles and integrated these in their own self-concept, depended not only on whether their mother was employed, but also on the extent to which fathers were involved in family work. A non-traditional distribution of labour between parents, with substantial paternal involvement in the family, was most conducive to non-sterotypical gender roles and to a commitment to role-sharing in the future that girls envisaged for themselves.

Boys, too, seeing more equal power relations in the home, are less likely to develop rigid masculine sex roles. There is also evidence that maternal employment may be related to superior adjustment in adolescent children, probably because of the greater ease with which employed mothers can grant independence.[16] Finally, recent research has begun to ask children themselves what they feel about mothers working. Far from considering themselves to be deprived, or 'latchkey children', some as young as 10 to 12, report that they enjoy coming home, usually with friends, to a 'vacant' house in which they enjoy time to themselves.[17] Clearly, the anxiety and guilt experienced by some mothers, and the prejudiced attitudes of some managers, associated with the belief that children will suffer if both parents are in employment, are misplaced.

CHILDCARE – WHO IS RESPONSIBLE?

Childcare is the most time and energy consuming of occupations. Childcare, unlike domestic work, cannot be neglected. It is not possible to cope with extra demands by lowering standards, and children cannot be swept under the carpet. Neither would dual-career couples wish to do so. Marilyn Rueschemeyer[18] interviewed dual-earner professional couples in the USA and Eastern bloc countries and concluded that these families tended to display a high level of commitment to both career and children. Professional couples expect their children to receive high quality attention, but the burden of responsibility for providing this care falls largely on mothers.

Dual-earner families have evolved some way from the traditional family structure and childcare is more likely than domestic work to be shared equally, but nevertheless career mothers often remain primary caretakers of children. Almost one half of the parents in our study said that they shared responsibility for childcare equally, which demonstrates a growing awareness of the importance of fathering. However, the majority of couples still felt that childcare was primarily the mother's job.

There are several reasons why dual-earner couples do not always share parenting equally, despite commitment to non-traditional ideology.

Social expectations
The prevailing view that mothers are mainly responsible for the care and well-being of children is influential. As discussed above, it makes mothers feel guilty if they share childcare with fathers or others. The social expectation that fathers ought not to be as involved as mothers in early childcare is also widely voiced:

> Some people find it hard to deal with the fact that I am so involved in the children's upbringing. When I took the baby for his injections, the woman doctor asked me if his mother was ill. (Community Worker, male)

Traditional gender expectations
Men who conform to traditional masculine stereotypes by being highly competitive and power oriented often feel that participating in childcare is too costly in career terms.[19] Similarly, women who conform to the traditional female role may be reluctant to relinquish their major responsibility for childcare.

Lack of role models
Many dual-earner spouses reared in traditional families are aware of a lack of role models for shared parenting:

> I never saw my father really involved with his children, so I think it's been a slow and painful learning experience for me. (Social Worker, male)

The impact of maternity leave
The availability of maternity leave, but not paternity or parental leave, may play an important role in shaping patterns of parenting:

> Obviously, I did most of the work while I was at home, the nappies, the washing and so on. We just seemed to carry on that way after I came back. And the baby seems to respond better to me. After all, I have been there all the time from the beginning. (Personnel Officer, female)

Organisational constraints
Managers and colleagues are often critical of men who wish to

reduce their involvement in work to make time to be with their children. A more socially acceptable pattern is for fathers to work harder putting in more overtime, when there are children to support. This 'breadwinner ethic' reduces the time and energy that fathers have available for childcare.

The advantages of shared parenting

The achievement of a more equal distribution of childcare responsibility is not only justified on the basis of fairness and egalitarianism. There is also evidence that paternal involvement in childcare benefits mothers, children and fathers themselves. Dual-earner mothers benefit by being less overloaded. Infants whose fathers are involved in their care have been found to be intellectually and socially more advanced.[20] Several studies of dual-earner families indicate that fathers who are involved in childcare enjoy better mental health than their less participative counterparts.[21] This may be because there is less pressure from their wives and an improved marital relationship. Many men also feel that they gain from their close relationship with their children.

Fathers who play a full part in childcare generally consider the rewards greater than the sacrifices, although these sacrifices can be substantial. Participant fathers interviewed by Lucia Gilbert,[22] were often prepared to limit their professional aspirations or to lengthen their timetables for achieving their goals. Mothers frequently do just this. Other fathers make smaller sacrifices but this also benefits the family:

> It stops me being as free as I might be at weekends, but I don't mind. Colleagues who don't have a working wife might go and play golf. I know I would get it in the neck if I did that. That's part of the contract, if you like. (Company Executive, male)

WHO CARES FOR THE CHILDREN WHEN BOTH PARENTS ARE AT WORK?

Pre-school children

Good childcare arrangements are crucial for dual-earner families. In countries where it is acceptable for mothers of young children to be employed outside the home, childcare poses no problems. Nursery places are widely available and affordable. In the UK pre-school childcare facilities are inadequate. Making childcare arrangements can be a major source of stress for new parents. Childcare arrangements have an important impact on parents' experiences of work and satisfactory provisions help to protect against the pressures of the two-earner lifestyle. Many mothers can only begin to derive satisfaction from their jobs if they are first satisfied with their childcare arrangements.[23]

A choice made by many couples with a sufficiently high joint income, is to employ a nanny or what is known as a 'mother's help' (indicating where parental duty is supposed to lie!) either on a live-in or on a daily basis. Opinions are divided as to whether living-in help is acceptable:

We wouldn't have a nanny living-in. There's no privacy. (Physician, female)

I think we will have somebody living-in until they leave school. Boarding school is definitely not the answer. The holidays are too long. (Company Executive, male)

Sometimes the decision to employ living-in help is reached as a last resort, after problems arise with other forms of childcare:

For the first child we had a series of arrangements. A childminder, then a nursery, but getting the baby out in the morning was such a rush. Then we had a series of people in on a daily basis and they kept leaving. When our second child was born, we gave in and employed a living-in nanny. It has made life much easier. (Physician, female)

In her study of dual-career couples working for large corporations, Rosanna Hertz[24] found that most parents preferred their children to be cared for by hired help at home because they believed that this situation, being nearest to the mother-child relationship, was preferable. She noted, however, that many families had problems, as nannies often did not stay for long, which was unsettling for the children. High turnover is typical of any job which requires few skills and offers few opportunities for advancement. Hertz argues that one reason for the high turnover of childcare help is that the pool from which they are drawn is a disadvantaged group, including young girls, older women and immigrants. She maintains that the solution is for professional childcare to be a well qualified, well paid and highly valued occupation, rather than the low status, poorly paid job which it often is. Most career couples recognise the logic of this. For couples who are able to pay a high salary and offer good conditions to suitably qualified people, turnover tends to be less of a problem.

We found that parents who employed a nanny or other home-based help experienced less stress than those using other forms of childcare. Nevertheless, many parents used childminders or nurseries, not only for financial reasons, but because they believe they provide opportunities for interaction with other children. A major difficulty with nurseries, however, is that the hours do not always coincide with parents' schedules. This problem can be resolved when a crèche is provided at the workplace of one of the parents. Those members of our survey fortunate enough to have such facilities generally found this very satisfactory.

The hospital nursery is indispensable to our way of life. (Radiologist, female)

It was upsetting at first leaving the baby at the nursery, but I was lucky I was able to take him in and stay the first couple of days and gradually reduce the time I stayed over a period of weeks. And Jane can pop in during the day and see him. (Salesman, married to Nurse using hospital nursery)

Given the lack of affordable childcare provision many couples rely on relatives to provide daytime childcare, but although this can be a satisfactory arrangement, it is not always forthcoming and it may strain family relationships.

My parents used to look after the baby, but I found we disagreed about a lot of things. I could tell someone else how I wanted him to be raised, but it wasn't easy to disagree with my parents – especially as I felt indebted to them. (Computer Consultant, female)

Finally, it should be noted that when parents, especially mothers, describe the advantages of various types of pre-school childcare arrangements, they are often defensive. For many mothers of young children, there is still an apparent need to justify the use of any substitute childcare:

The other two weren't as small when I left them. Perhaps I felt a bit guilty in those days, but now I realise that the baby is quite happy. It doesn't matter as long as you can trust the person you leave them with. Even women who don't work spend a lot of time going out shopping, playing golf or going to coffee mornings. (Lawyer, female)

School-aged children

Once children start school, women who felt uneasy about continuing their career feel more comfortable, and indeed many women do not return to work until this stage. However, there are new problems as school hours do not fit in with the hours of most full-time employment. Parents have to reorganise their lives so that they, or someone else, can collect the children from school:

> It's much more difficult now she is at school. She has to be picked up at 3.30. The childminder was much more flexible. I could collect her at 5.30 or 6. (Theatrical Agent, female)

As well as the time between the end of school and the end of the working day, school holidays also create a problem. Some schools run after-school programmes, and there are various play schemes and camps for children in the holidays. Parents also rely on more informal support from friends and family, but making these arrangements can be stressful.

Parents may also face difficulties in living up to the expectations of teachers and schoolchildren. Again, the pressure to meet these expectations is more often experienced by mothers, although many fathers are also aware of the problem:

> Sometimes it's a problem when the children have to have a fancy dress for school. I mean, there just isn't time to make elaborate fancy dresses like other mothers do, so I feel my kids miss out. (Paediatrician, female)

> There are events at school to which parents are invited, often at short notice. It's difficult for either of us to be there, but we do try our best if we have time to arrange things, because we know other children will have a parent there. (Dentist, male)

In part, this problem arises because schools' expectations of parents' availability may be unrealistic. It can also be argued, however, that there is a justifiable expectation that jobs should be more flexible in order to allow parents the space to have some involvement in children's school lives. Some modification in the expectations of both schools and employers would help to avoid these conflicts.

WHO STAYS AT HOME IN A CRISIS?

Even if there are well organised regular childcare arrangements with back-up systems, there is always the potential for something to go wrong. When a child is too ill to go to nursery or school, the nanny or babysitter is ill and friends and relatives are not available, it may be necessary for one parent to remain at home. The question then arises, who is going to cancel appointments or interrupt their work?

We asked dual-earner parents the question, 'Who would be more likely to take time off work in a domestic crisis?' Just under 30 per cent responded that it would depend upon which parent was most busy at work and 7 per cent said it would be the father. Over 60 per cent of couples maintained that the mother would be the one most likely to take time off. So when childcare crises arise, the father's worklife is much less likely to be disrupted than the mother's, reinforcing the stereotype of working mothers as 'unreliable'. Social expectations clearly play a large part in perpetuating this situation. It is often difficult for men to take time off without their professional commitment being called into question. However, many women were determined not to allow children to interfere with their work at any cost, for fear of being seen to conform to the female stereotype:

> I feel that I have to work harder and perform better than male colleagues or colleagues without young children. It's as though I am on trial. There is no way I could take time off if one of the kids was sick. It would just reinforce the general prejudices. (Product Manager, mother of two)

Schools and nurseries also play a part in reinforcing this view of the mother's responsibility for children. If children become ill at school, parents must be contacted. It is a frequent complaint that although both parents leave their telephone number in case a child becomes ill, it is invariably the mother who is contacted first and who must disrupt her work:

> The school has both our numbers but if Jonathon is ill they always phone me. On one occasion I was in a lecture and found a message when I returned to my office. I phoned the school just to check that they had managed to contact my husband, but they hadn't even tried. The secretary said she didn't like to bother him. The really infuriating thing is that my husband is a school governor and they think nothing of contacting him if the roof is leaking or something like that, but not because his child is ill. (Lecturer, female)

Social policy also mitigates against fathers taking their share of work disruption due to childcare crises. In the UK there is no national provision for paid sick leave to take care of a child, although some organisations do provide this facility. Unpaid leave is more likely to be taken by the mother except in the minority of cases where she earns the higher income, because it is both more socially acceptable and would be less costly. If paid leave were available for either parent, this might legitimise the taking of leave for family reasons and lead to greater equality in terms of which parent stays at home.

Despite the powerful influence of social expectations, many men do take an equal, or even greater, share of responsibility for dealing with childcare crises. For people who are highly committed to their careers, it is rarely an easy decision to drop everything and stay at home, but neither is it always easy to leave a sick child. When both parents have busy schedules, a crisis of this nature can cause considerable conflict. A psychologist and mother of two described how she and her partner had attempted to deal with such a contingency:

> This is something we planned and talked about; the potential conflict between our jobs if the children were sick. We arranged that we would just divide the week into two without any arguments. If a child was sick and someone had to stay with her in the first part of the week, then one of us would take time off, irrespective of what was going on at work and vice versa for the second half of the week. In practice, of course, there was more discussion on individual days, because some days one of us would have very little to do and it would be silly to be inflexible. But it did mean that in principle if one of us didn't have a lot pencilled in our diary on a particular day, we weren't obliged to be the one at home. And it avoided arguments about whose work is more important.

An important point made by many parents is that childcare crises are just that; crises by and large, do not happen frequently. In the normal run of events, parents' working time suffers the minimum of disruption, although as with employees' own illnesses, crises are unpredictable. Even in difficult circumstances, however, dual-earner parents usually manage to cope, often much better than their employers expect. This is illustrated by the case of Julia, a lawyer in a large organisation and Graeme, also a lawyer, who have a disabled child. Julia's employers anticipated that this would cause particular disruption to her career and were sympathetic about this but, as she explained, they were mistaken:

> I have a mentally disabled child and worry about him a great deal. This doesn't have to interfere with my work, though. I find that the more responsible and onerous duties are not asked of me, partly out of a misplaced sense of kindness and over-protectiveness on the part of my superiors and partly, I suspect, because I am not expected to be reliable.

CARE OF ELDERLY PARENTS AND OTHER RELATIVES

We are living in an ageing society. The European Commission has predicted that by the end of this century one in four people in most member states will be over the age of 60.[25] Nevertheless, the issue of eldercare – the care of elderly or sick relatives – has received little attention to date. Government commitment to limiting public spending and encouraging care within the community exacerbates what may become a huge issue for dual-earner families. Traditionally, care in the community has been provided by daughters or daughters-in-law who, having completed their childcare responsibilities, move on to the next phase of caring. This assumes that these women do not work. In Japan, where the population has aged even more rapidly than in the West and where there is a strong tradition of the eldest son (or rather his wife) caring for the elderly, eldercare now presents a problem of even greater proportion than childcare for dual-earner families.[26] It is also potentially a huge problem for dual-earner couples and their employers in this country.[27] Without adequate public or corporate support, it is generally women's careers which are interrupted or curtailed. Many of the women and a few of the men we interviewed were aware of this as a potential problem, or experienced guilt and conflict similar to that experienced by some mothers of young children as they attempted to balance paid work and caring responsibilities. Others had disabled children and worried about what they would do when they left school, as cuts in public expenditure had reduced the services available to them:[28]

> There's uncertainty because we don't know what the future's going to be. There is no legal necessity to provide anything for these young people with disabilities after they

are 19 – so she may have to stay at home, and I'll have to stay at home and look after her.

WHAT CAN ORGANISATIONS DO?

Childcare provision

Difficulty in making childcare arrangements is the primary obstacle to women in the UK returning to work after maternity leave.[29] The state provision of childcare for the under-fives is inadequate, while private nurseries and nannies are expensive and accessible only to a minority. There is, therefore, ample scope for organisations to develop childcare initiatives. Childcare is not a luxury perk, but a necessity to enable dual-career spouses to work.

Below, we discuss some of the options available to organisations to alleviate employees' childcare problems. Some of these benefits are offered by a growing number of organisations in the UK. Other initiatives have been pioneered in the USA by organisations responding to the needs of working parents, or elsewhere in Europe, where there is a growing recognition that successful management increasingly depends on enabling employees to reconcile their work and family responsibilities.[30]

Workplace nurseries

Traditionally, workplace nurseries have been provided in organisations, such as hospitals, which employ large numbers of highly trained women and recognise the importance of accommodating their childcare needs. More recently, the need for such facilities has been recognised in a wider range of organisations. Unlike other forms of childcare provision, workplace nurseries are not taxed as an employee perk. This applies whether they are on- or off-site and also to nurseries run jointly with other companies, or with local authorities, providing that the premises are made available by one or more of the participants, and the employer providing the exempt benefits is wholly or partly responsible for financing and managing the provision. The cost of setting up and running a workplace nursery is often considered to be prohibitive but this should be seen as a benefit in kind similar to, and equally essential as, a canteen or sports and social clubs. Furthermore workplace nurseries have been shown to have economic as well as qualitative benefits.[31] Savings were calculated in terms of recruitment and retraining due to the dramatic rise in the numbers of women returning after maternity leave, as well as the benefits of reduced stress, decline in absenteeism and improved timekeeping.

On-site childcare or a nursery located near to the place of work has several advantages over other forms of childcare. Parents are able to see their children during the day and are readily available in an emergency. Crèches are invaluable for mothers who return to work while still breastfeeding. The hours of a workplace nursery coincide with those of the working day, avoiding the problems of incompatible schedules. On-site childcare makes life much easier for parents and this is reflected in improved performance and satisfaction, a better working climate and lower turnover. Despite these substantial benefits, however, there are also limitations to workplace nurseries. Employees who commute long distances to work may prefer a childcare facility nearer to home because of the difficulties of travelling with the child. Clearly, workplace nurseries can be invaluable under some circumstances, but in other situations, such as when a company draws personnel from a wide range of locations, it might also be worthwhile considering other options.

Childcare consortia

Many employers reject the notion of a workplace nursery on the grounds that the number of employees with young children is too small to justify such a provision. However, the need for childcare still exists for parents employed in smaller organisations. One strategy is for an organisation to set up a nursery, giving priority to its own employees, while also providing places for employees of neighbouring companies, who would contribute to the cost. Another way of increasing demand and spreading the cost is for a number of employers in close proximity, or drawing from a workforce in a common residential area, to form a consortium to share the provision of a nursery.

Working with local government

The number of state nurseries has declined dramatically with recent cuts in public spending. The business community can work together with local government by contributing funds to enable established nurseries to remain open, or those which have been forced to close down to re-open. When planning permission for a new office development on behalf of stockbrokers Merrill Lynch was sought, the local council, Islington, required that childcare facilities should be included as part of planning gain. The result was the opening of the City Child Nursery in January

1988 in the heart of London's financial centre. The pooling of local authorities' childcare expertise and private sector financial resources may well lead to other joint ventures of this nature.

Other financial benefits
A growing number of organisations in the UK now provide employees with childcare allowances. Direct financial contributions towards childcare, or childcare vouchers, although taxable, increase parents' choices. Money or vouchers can be used to fund a nursery place or childminder, or as a contribution towards the cost of a nanny, or paying a relative. Alternatively, some employers contract with existing private childcare facilities, offering discount on childcare fees to their employees. Arrangements include the subsidy of 'slots' of places in a nursery. Employers guarantee payment for a number of places and these are reserved for company employees. Other firms operate a voucher system. This is a subsidy provided by the organisation to its employees to enable them to purchase childcare from any recognised nursery or childminder.

Cafeteria-style benefits
Not all employees require the same benefits and the needs of individuals change over time. Dual-earner spouses with young children need assistance with childcare, but the requirements of those with older children and the single and the childfree are different. In order to meet the needs of a diversity of families at different lifestages, some companies in the USA have introduced cafeteria-style benefits. Employees select for themselves the benefits they wish to have from a wide menu of choice. These might include childcare benefits, insurance, more vacation time or days off. This is a good way of increasing employees' involvement in the decision-making process, enabling them to tailor the benefits offered to their own specific needs at a particular time, and ensuring equity for those without children.

In addition to providing childcare on-site and/or assisting with off-site childcare for the under-fives, there are several other ways in which organisations can reduce stress for dual-career parents.

Information and referral service
New parents or parents newly resident in a particular location can benefit from a service providing information about local childcare services. This would include lists of nurseries, childminders and agencies providing nannies and other in-home help.

Several organisations have found this to be a relatively inexpensive, but nevertheless valuable, service. A childcare advisor employed by the organisation is also invaluable.

Paid leave to care for a sick child
It is imperative that organisations formulate a policy on sick children, to complement childcare policies. Most European states have legislation granting employees the right to some paid leave for pressing family reasons. Britain has yet to act on this. Nevertheless, a few organisations do provide paid leave for a specific maximum period to care for a sick child. If this benefit is made available to both parents, it would encourage the sharing of childcare responsibilities and the leave taken by any single employee would be unlikely to be excessive.

Alternative arrangements for the care of sick children
Although paid leave to care for a sick child should be available, it must be recognised that many employers are reluctant or unable to drop everything to cope with this situation. A number of alternative policies which have been implemented by pioneering organisations in Europe and the US to help parents cope with a sick child without taking time off work have been found to be cost effective.[32] They include the following:

- In-home sick childcare service. Trained nurses or caregivers are sent to the child's own home when he/she is too ill to attend a nursery, or if the regular caregiver is ill.
- Mildly ill children may be cared for in a special room or wing of a workplace crèche, or in a hospital wing.
- In Berkeley, California, a satellite sick childcare programme has been set up, called '*Wheezles and Sneezles*'. This is located adjacent to a childcare centre and is staffed by the same caregivers, so that they are familiar to the children. It is visited by healthy children, so that if and when they have to use it, it is not a strange environment.

Parents who take time off for domestic crises report feeling guilty about letting down clients or customers. A 'locum' or 'supply' system of temporary staff to cover their absences would reduce this pressure.

After-school programmes
Childcare problems do not disappear once a child begins school. In some ways the situation becomes more difficult, as the length of the school day is shorter than the working day. Organisations

can assist by arranging to transport children from schools to their parents' workplace and many companies also provide after-school childcare programmes. School holidays can also present a problem for children too old to attend a nursery, but too young to be left at home alone. Organisations or groups of organisations could assist by offering holiday childcare or summer groups for employees' children. These are exempt from tax. Perhaps more fundamentally, it is important that parents are given the opportunity to take their vacation to coincide with school holidays. Flexible working arrangements can be used to enable parents to work longer in term-time and so save up time to allow them a longer break during school holidays. Term-time working contracts are also increasingly popular.

Parenting seminars
Parent education can also be taken seriously by organisations. Some employers sponsor workshops at the workplace to address parenting issues ranging from the balancing of care of young children with a career, to dealing with schools or recognising substance abuse in teenagers. Sometimes known as 'brown bag seminars' these are usually held during the lunch-hour. As with all the initiatives described in this section, these seminars should be available for both mothers and fathers, and should not be seen as only applicable to women.

Assistance with eldercare and other family care

Much of what has been said about the problems of caring for young children also applies to employees who have responsibilities for elderly parents or for other sick or disabled relatives. Organisations which are genuinely committed to accommodating the link between work and family need to take these reponsibilities into account. This may be achieved through the provision of company daycare centres for the elderly or infirm, by subsidising places at other centres, by providing a number of days' paid leave, or making nursing staff available to visit the employees' home in emergencies.

In the US, where eldercare is described as the 'perk' of the 1990s,[33] one shoe company has combined eldercare with childcare[34] and some European companies have experimented with placing childcare facilities in homes for the elderly. In addition, extended periods of paid or unpaid leave or sabbaticals are useful to enable employees to spend more time with relatives in extreme situations, such as during a terminal illness. The stoical presence in the workplace of employees with anxieties and guilt about close relatives benefits neither the individuals nor the organisations and the problems will not go away simply because organisations refuse to acknowledge that they exist. Some companies have found that policies such as reduced hours or career breaks introduced to help with childcare, have been used by those with other caring responsibilities, and this has alerted them to the issue.

Provisions for respite care, for the elderly and disabled, can give employees with caring responsibilities a much-needed break. The multinational glassmakers, Pilkingtons, has a separate charitable organisation, funded by a trust, which provides a wide range of services for its pensioners, as well as for elderly or sick realtives of employees, who might otherwise be unable to work. The services provided include respite care, sending people into employees' homes to relieve carers, home meals and laundry.

REFERENCES

1. Groves, V (1987) *The Complete Woman*, London: Chatto and Windus.
2. Sekaran, U (1985) 'The paths to mental health: An exploratory study of husbands and wives in dual career families', *Journal of Occupational Psychology*, 58, 2, 129–138.
3. Greenhous, J H and Kopelman, R E (1981) 'Conflict between work and non-work roles. Implications for the career planning process', *Human Resource Planning*, 4, 1–10.
4. Russo, N F (1979) 'Overview: sex roles, fertility and the motherhood mandate', *Psychology of Women Quarterly*, 4, 1, 7–15.
5. Walker, L J and Walker, J L (1980) 'Trait anxiety in mothers. Differences associated with employment status, family, size and age of children', *Psychological Reports*, 67, 295–299.
6. Gilbert, L A, Holohan, C K and Manning, L (1981) 'Coping with conflict between professional and maternal roles', *Family Relations*, 30, 419–426.
7. Bowlby, J (1953) *Childcare and the Growth of Love*, Harmondsworth: Penguin.
8. Rutter, M (1981) *Maternal Deprivation Reassessed*, Harmondsworth: Penguin.
9. Jowell, R, Witherspoon, S and Brook, L (eds) (1988) *British Social Attitudes: the Fifth Report*, Aldershot: Gower.
10. Lewis, S and Cooper, C L (1983) 'The stress of combining

occupational and parental roles: A review of the literature', *Bulletin of the British Psychological Society*, 36, 341–345.

11. Hoffman, L W (1989) 'Effects of maternal employment in the two parent family', *American Psychologist*, 44, 283–292.

12. Hoffman, L W (1989) op cit.

13. Hoffman, L W (1989) op cit.

14. Sandburg, D F, Ehrhardt, A A, Mellins, C A, Ince, S E and Meyer-Bahjburg, H F L (1987) 'The influence of individual and family characteristics on career aspirations of girls during childhood and adolescence', *Sex Roles*, 16, 649–667.

15. Gilbert, L A and Dancer, L S (1992) 'Dual Earner Families in the United States and Adolescent Development', in S Lewis, D N Izraeli and H Hootsmans (eds), *Dual Earner Families, International Perspectives*, Sage, London.

16. Gold, D and Andres, D (1978) Comparisons of adolescent children with employed or non employed mothers. *Merrill Palmer Quarterly*, 24, 4, 243–254.

17. Solberg, A (1990) 'Negotiating childhood: changing constructions of age for Norwegian children', in A James and A Prout (eds), *Constructing and Reconstructing Childhood*, Falmer Press, London.

18. Rueschemeyer, M (1981) *Professional Work and Marriage. An East West Comparison*, Macmillan, London.

19. Gilbert, L A (1985) *Men in Dual Career Families, Current Realities and Future Perspectives*, Lawrence Erlbaum, Hillsdale, N J.

20. Carro, G (1983) 'Stay home fathers' superkids', *Psychology Today*, 17, 71.

21. Pleck, J H (1985) *Working Wives/Working Husbands*, Beverly Hills, Sage, California.

22. Gilbert, L A (1985) op cit.

23. Harrell, J E and Ridley, C A (1975) 'Substitute childcare, maternal employment and the quality of mother-child interaction', *Journal of Marriage and the Family*, 27, 556–563.

24. Hertz, R (1986) *More Equal than Others: Men and Women in Dual Career Marriages*, Berkeley, University of California Press.

25. Berry-Lound, D (1990) *Work and Family, Carer Friendly Employment Practices*, London: Institute of Personnel Management.

26. Chabot, J T (1992) 'Dual Earner Families and The Care of the Elderly in Japan, in S Lewis, D N Izraeli and H Hootsman (eds), op cit.

27. Davidson, M and Cooper, C (1992) *Shattering the Glass Ceiling*, Paul Chapman, London.
28. Kagan, C and Lewis, S (1993) 'Family, employment and social change in Britain, accounts of women with multiple commitments'. Paper presented at a Committee on Family Research Conference on Rapid Social Change in the Family, Palango, Lithuania.
29. Daniel, W W (1980) *Maternity Rights, The Experience of Women*, London: Policy Studies Unit.
30. Hogg, C and Harker, L (1992) *The Family Friendly Employer: Examples from Europe*, London: The Daycare Trust.
31. Truman, C (1986) *Overcoming the Career Break, A Positive Approach*, Sheffield: Manpower Services Commission.
32. Kamerman, S B and Kahn, A J (1987) *The Responsive Workplace, Employers and a Changing Workforce*, New York: Columbia University Press.
33. Friedman, D E and Grey, W B (1989) *A Life Cycle Approach To Family Benefits and Policies*, New York: Conference Board.
34. Hootsmans, H 'Dutch and British Corporations and the Challenge of Dual Career Couples', in S Lewis, D N Izraeli and H Hootsmans (eds) op cit.

6
Working Together

Members of dual-earner couples work together as partners, albeit not always equal ones, in the home, and in producing family income. Are changing gender roles and relationships in the family reflected in a greater understanding and equality between men and women in the wider sphere of the workplace? In this chapter, we explore some of the dynamics of dual-earner spouses' working relationships in the home, and of the working relationships of men and women in the workplace. We also consider some implications for organisations.

WORKING TOGETHER IN THE HOME

A recent survey by the Family Policies Study Centre[1] indicated that 73 per cent of women in the UK do nearly all the housework, and that men in dual-earner households have an average of six hours' more spare time at weekends than their wives. Our research bore out these findings. We asked husbands and wives about their responsibility for housework, including shopping, cleaning, cooking, laundry, and for maintenance tasks, which included the more traditional male tasks of household repairs and gardening. Although approximately one quarter of the women and one third of the men claimed that they shared responsibility for housework, the remainder reported that this was regarded as the wife's responsibility. The trend was reversed for maintenance tasks. Men were seen, and saw themselves, as carrying major responsibility in this area. Less than a quarter of respondents claimed that responsibility was shared. Thus, the 'new man' who participates equally in running the home and, indeed, the 'new woman' who does her share of household maintenance, do exist, but a traditional division of domestic responsibility prevails for the majority of couples. It is the domestic chores which need performing on a routine day to day basis, thus increasing daily overload, which fall mainly upon women.

Childcare responsibility tended to be more equally shared than domestic tasks (see Chapter 5). This finding is consistent with a growing body of evidence that fathers in dual-career families are becoming increasingly involved in childcare.[2] This involvement, however, tends to be limited to the more pleasurable aspects, such as playing with their children, rather than tidying up after them and performing the more mundane chores.[3] It seems that many men give intellectual support to their wives' careers, but practical support, in terms of participation in family work, is not always forthcoming.

Spillover of domestic work

Domestic overload can spill over to affect the experience of work. Men may have less difficulty than women in switching off from the family while they are at work, as it is usually wives who plan and organise the household and children. Most husbands merely return home to perform the tasks allocated to them. Thus women often find domestic matters intruding into their thoughts during the day:

> In the middle of a lecture I might suddenly remember we have no toilet paper in the house, or when I'm in a meeting I might find myself wondering what we will have for dinner. How many men do that? Most of them have it all organised for them. (Lecturer, female)

Even among couples who do share domestic responsibility, there are often areas of work in which men do not participate, partly because they have the ability to switch off from family matters during the day. A social worker whose partner participated fairly equally in childcare pointed out that there were still differences in the way they approached the children's needs:

> If I pass a shop with children's things in, I might go in and buy something we need. I suppose, if the girls actually had no knickers, that might compel John to go and look for some, but otherwise he has never bought children's clothes and wouldn't know where to go. I think it's because I think ahead and I carry these things around with me all the time. Possibly it's a different way of thinking. I think in parallel much more than John does. He thinks in serial, one thing after another.

In some cases the spillover of domestic concerns to the workplace can prevent women from gaining maximum satisfaction from their work. In our study, we found that women who had the most domestic responsibility were more likely than others to report that they were dissatisfied with their job. This may be partly because of a desire for more flexibility, or for shorter working hours, so as to fit in domestic work, but it may also be because they were unable to give full attention to their job. This interference from the domestic front may prevent some women from achieving as much as they would like to in terms of promotion, recognition or simply having the satisfaction of a job well done.

Social pressures: responsibility versus performance of tasks

One major factor contributing to the continuing unequal division of domestic labour is that many dual-earner couples still accept, at a conscious or unconscious level, the cultural definition of housework as a 'prior commitment' of a woman, whether or not she is in paid employment. Thus, although both sexes accept the wife's right to a career, it is often women who feel responsible if domestic work is neglected.

> Of course we believe that housework should be shared equally between us, but it is me who feels guilty if the net curtains look dirty when someone comes in. (Teacher, female)

The distinction between taking responsibility for domestic work and merely performing certain tasks, is an important one. Performance of tasks requires physical activity, but responsibility requires skills of a different nature, including planning, delegation, supervision and problem solving. Rhona and Robert Rapoport, in their studies of dual-career families,[4] described the *sense of responsibility* for domestic work as one of the key bottlenecks to sex role changes and real equality in marriage. They pointed out that a shift in perceptions of responsibility requires not only an alteration in behaviour, but also a significant change to 'maps in the head'. The deep-seated belief that household chores are really women's work, and that dual-earner husbands 'help' in the house, even if the 'help' is substantial, constructs women as managers of the home with men as, at best, their assistants. It is not a management role that men are clamouring to take over at present.

> Malcolm is very good. He helps with all the housework, washing and cooking. He'll do anything I ask him. (Biologist)

The notion that a man's contribution to housework constitutes 'help' creates difficulty for some women, who feel guilty about asking for assistance or angry about having to do so. One female manager blamed herself because she felt unable to ask her husband for help, even though she was comfortable in delegating and sharing responsibility at work, where the guidelines were much clearer:

> It's not that he doesn't want to help, I think it's something in me. If the roles were reversed, I couldn't just sit and watch him make the dinner. I don't like having to tell him what to do. I'd like him to do it on his own initiative. If he just came and started preparing the veg I would be happy, but rather than ask him I do it myself.

Many couples delegate a substantial amount of their domestic chores to hired help. Nevertheless, the sense that housework is primarily the wife's responsibility, and that paid help enables her to delegate her burden rather than reducing a workload that is the responsibility of both spouses, prevails:

> I pay someone else to do the housework. In fact, everything domestic that I can delegate, I do. I mean I could do it, but it's finding the time. (Chartered Accountant, female)

> I'm more responsible for organising the running of the home, so therefore what I can't do, I pay help to do. (Social Worker, female)

Surprisingly, research has found that the tendency to share responsibility, or to divide domestic responsibility according to gender, is not consistently related to views about gender roles.[5] Those people who hold non-traditional views about the roles of women and men in the wider society do not necessarily translate these attitudes into behaviour in the home. It seems to be easier to reject cultural definitions of masculine and feminine behaviour intellectually, and to put it into practice in career terms, than it is to change things in the home. This can cause some discomfort for those who recognise the incongruence between their belief in equality and their actual behaviour:

> I know I don't really pull my weight at home and I do feel bad about it. We both believe in equality and often talk about it and decide to change things, but then we just slide back into old habits. (Engineer, male)

> I am aware that childcare is likely to be a problem. I like to

think that we are both sufficiently liberated to share child-care when the time comes, but I am aware of the power of social expectations. At the moment I'm afraid it's easier for me to tidy the kitchen and for John to tidy the garage, in spite of our liberated views. I don't like it, though, and I'm determined not to give in over childcare. (Personnel Manager, female)

This belief that domestic work is a fundamental responsibility of women prevents many dual-earner wives from expressing dis-satisfaction with their unequal load. We asked both women and men if they were satisfied with their spouse's contribution to domestic work. Not surprisingly, women were more likely than men to feel that their partner did not do his fair share. Mothers of young children, who have the greatest domestic workload, tended to be more dissatisfied with their partner's contribution. Nevertheless, the majority of women reported feeling fairly satisfied, even though they carried the major responsibility for household work. For many there was a resigned acceptance of their greater workload:

I do the bulk of the cleaning. Mike does his own ironing, he washes up and he'll hoover. He's very good really. But the bulk of the cleaning, the floors, the bathroom and toilet, are mine. Basically, it's because I notice it, but I don't make a big thing of it. It's not a source of friction. (Theatrical Agent)

When I'm cleaning the lavatory on a Sunday afternoon, I think this is enough. But I know it's the same for all working women with kids. They are all cleaning the lavatory on a Sunday afternoon. (Nurse)

Even those women who are dissatisfied often express this in terms of wanting a little more help, rather than wanting the work to be shared equally:

I would like a bit more help. The agreement was that when I went back to full-time work it was on the condition that I had more help. As it turns out the actual additional contribution he makes is to empty the dishwasher. I thought the balance would be a bit different, but it hasn't worked out that way.

THE CONCEPT OF EQUITY

Why do women accept this situation? The Rapoports[6] proposed that the extent to which dual-career spouses express satisfaction with their work in the home will depend upon whether they believe the situation to be equitable. The notion of equity is more subjective than equality, which refers to how much actual work is performed by each partner. Why should unequal loads be perceived as being equitable, or fair? Judgments of what is equitable in the family context depend not only on the actual time spent in homemaking and paid work by each spouse, but also on the attitudes towards assumed, gender-related responsibilities, and the value of each partner's contribution in each domain. As long as men's household work is regarded as voluntary help, even a small amount will be valued and women will be relatively satisfied to carry the major load. This can lead to some fairly irrational assessments of the situation!

> I know I do more in the house than Andrew, but I can't grumble because he does his fair share. (Careers Officer)

It is also part of the stereotypical feminine role for a wife to be supportive towards her husband in his career, listening to his problems and offering consolation for disappointments. Traditionally, women do not expect this type of emotional support from husbands, but it is increasingly provided by men in dual-career marriages.[7] However, because this support is not taken for granted, some women feel that it compensates for more practical support in the form of household work:

> I don't think that the important thing is the physical factor of how much my husband does at home, but more the psychological factor, supportiveness. He recognises my career as being no less important than his and I think that is what really counts. (Training Officer)

Social and organisational barriers to men's participation in housework

So far we have focused on the impact of social norms on women, but men in dual-career families are also constrained by social expectations. Although society is still ambivalent about mothers of young children remaining in the workforce, women do now receive some encouragement to enter what were once traditional male areas of work. Men have received much less encouragement to expand their domestic participation.[8] Men who do wish to share family work equally, often find this difficult to reconcile with the expectations of their employers and others:

If I tell my colleagues that I cannot attend a lunchtime gathering because I have to do the shopping, I am ridiculed. My firm often expects me to go in at weekends, which is when we usually catch up with the washing and housework at home. I can't say that I can't go in because I have housework to do. They would think I was crazy. I don't think I do my fair share at home but I am certainly not happy with the situation. (Engineer)

Evidence is emerging to suggest that men who have an egalitarian relationship with a career wife suffer less stress than those who cling to a more inappropriate division of labour.[9,10] Organisational constraints which prevent men from taking their share of family work may thus be a source of stress.

WORKING TOGETHER GENERATING FAMILY INCOME

One important factor which helps to determine what is considered to be fair in terms of family work is the relative income of each spouse. In this country, as elsewhere, average male earnings remain higher than average female earnings. This is partly a consequence of discrimination, the lower pay attached to traditionally female-dominated work, and also because women's prior commitment to family work often means they are less likely to work overtime than men. Many couples feel that the husband's greater earning power justifies his lesser contribution to domestic work. As one male sales manager put it:

My career finances the family. Well, obviously I get satisfaction out of doing it, but the reason I work is to support the family. Elaine earns much less than I do, so it's right that she should shoulder more of the responsibility for the house and children.

Similarly, a female manager recognised her husband as the major breadwinner, in spite of her substantial financial contribution, and therefore accepted her greater domestic responsibility:

He earns a lot more than I do and his work is very demanding. He's too busy to do housework. I'm quite happy with the arrangement. I accept it. I've always believed his career was uppermost.

In accepting greater domestic load because of their lower earnings, women may reduce their opportunities for promotion, and hence perpetuate the 'earnings gap'. Household work tends to be measured in terms of time expended, while paid work is assessed in terms of earnings and the significance of each partner's earnings for the family's standard of living.[11] Myra Ferree, in her study of the 'superwoman syndrome', noted that women who are the major breadwinner in their family have more power in the marital relationship, and are more likely than other women to demand greater participation from their husbands in the home.[12] She found that although women with a feminist consciousness, who earn less than their spouse, might do less housework than other women, it is because they lower their standards rather than demand more participation from their partners. Many of these women continue to perform more of the work than their husbands, and do not necessarily see this as unfair. Women's ability to earn as much or more than their husbands seems to be more powerful than non-sexist attitudes alone in changing patterns of behaviour at home.

All this implies that the path to greater equality at home lies in policies which will help to enhance women's earning power. Although this is undoubtedly true, changes in attitudes towards the financial contributions of women and men are also necessary. Many dual-career couples regard the wife's income as expendable even if it is equal to, or greater than, the husband's. This is because she might take a career break for childcare at some stage, while he is expected to earn continuously.

> Alison earns more than I do at the moment, but in a few years' time maybe she will want to work part-time, if we have children. Obviously, we have to think of my job as being the most important. (Radiologist, male)

The majority of dual-career wives may not be the major breadwinners, but they do, nevertheless, make a substantial contribution to the family income. Women's earnings tend to be undervalued due to the belief that their contribution is expendable and that domestic work and childcare are women's primary responsibility. In a study of dual-earner couples in which the wife had recently returned from maternity leave,[13] Julia Brannen and Peter Moss found that women contributed 42 per cent of the family income, but that it was usually women who paid for items such as childcare and domestic help. As employment is often regarded as an option for the woman, additional to her primary domestic commitment, many couples do not consider the wife's

actual contribution to the family income, but only what is left
after she has paid for those items which allow her (as opposed to
allowing both parents) to work:

> Really, it's hardly worth my while working. By the time I've
> paid the nanny and the cleaner, there isn't a great deal left, so
> I really work for career satisfaction rather than purely
> financial reasons. (Chemist, female)

Since fathers are expected to work and to be breadwinners, their
full income is often compared with women's income after paying
for domestic outgoings. This makes the income differential seem
much greater than it is. Both income differentials between the
sexes, and underlying attitudes towards the responsibilities of
women and men which devalue women's financial contributions
to the family, help to explain why many men continue to participate less than their wives in domestic work and why women
often accept this situation as satisfactory, despite adverse effects
on their own career.

Thus, just as many dual-earner spouses work together in traditional ways in the home – she as manager, he as assistant – so,
too, the task of producing the family income is often shared along
traditional lines. Inevitably, though, as women advance in their
careers, this traditional pattern of income generation is being
challenged, with more women becoming equal or main breadwinners. In these times of transition between the highly traditional marriages of the past and the emerging egalitarian
relationships, these changes often raise new issues and create
new tensions.

In partnerships where the husband's earnings and status are
higher than the wife's, the traditional division of labour may
remain intact. Increasingly, dual-career marriages are deviating
from this pattern. Some men increase their domestic responsibilities, in order to support their wives' careers, often reducing
their own career aspirations. However, men who are ambivalent
about their new roles find it more difficult to relinquish long-
standing attitudes and to accept that their wives' careers and
occupational demands are as, if not more, important than their
own. Husbands may begin to feel that they are in competition
with their wives, and this can create stress and tension within the
relationship. The real challenge to a couple's ability to adapt to
changing marital roles occurs when the normative pattern is
reversed. When wives achieve higher occupational status and/or
salary, and have higher career commitment and aspirations than

their husbands, particularly in traditionally male fields,[14] this can create considerable tension in men who are ambivalent about evolving de-gendered roles.[15]

Men who are aware of the impact of gender expectations are less threatened by their wives' success, but those who cling to more traditional expectations, believing that the provider role defines their masculinity, often find this threatening. If their wife no longer depends upon them for financial support, they may feel that they are no longer needed and fear an imminent breakdown of their marriage. A female manager illustrated the problem when she described the problems created by her career success during her previous marriage:

> He resented my success and that I was more successful than he was. I earned more than him and consequently I had my independence. He resented that. He kept going on about my having affairs with people at work. It wasn't true, not for want of the chance, but I wasn't interested. The more successful I became, the worse things were.

While many marriages break up as a consequence of the wife's success, other women change to a job of inferior status or lower their aspirations in order to reduce the threat to their husband's ego.[16] A Further Education lecturer confessed:

> I could have gone much further in my career but I know that James would have felt the need to compete with me and there would have been murder at home. It wasn't worth it. My marriage is more important.'

When this happens, marriage serves to prevent women from reaching their full potential. Career aspirations and commitment are important factors protecting dual-career men and women against stress.[16] By reducing or denying aspirations, women may appear to be saving their marriages, but they may also be creating other forms of stress for themselves, as they pave the way for a lifetime of non-stretching work.

It is not only men who have difficulty in adapting to equality in marriage with all its implications. Some women also feel more comfortable in a marriage where the husband's occupation is dominant and the wife, however successful, remains dependent upon him:

> I've been married before and learned from the experience.

It's different with Robert. He's more intelligent. He's a man I can lean on. (Personnel Manager)

Ellen Berman and her associates[17] suggest that couples who meet during their professional training initially believe that they have a marriage between equals, but often both partners retain the cultural assumption of male superiority, at a subconscious level. As the wife develops professionally and earns as much as, or more than, her husband, she expects at a conscious level that they will be equals (her new ideals) while demanding, often unconsciously, that her husband be her superior (her old conditioning). Women want equality, but they often find it difficult to escape from their early socialisation:

> You are brought up as a child to think that Father goes out to work and Mother stays at home, or works a little when she wants to. I'm a little envious of women who don't have to work, in the sense that they don't have the pressure of being the major wage earner. (Physician, female)

> I love my work. I like the money. But it's difficult not to model yourself on your parents. I earn more than my husband, so I don't follow that model. I think that's quite stressful. (Lawyer, female)

Women struggling to come to terms with social expectations, internalised during childhood, tend to articulate beliefs about equality, and to be reluctant to acknowledge these deeper conflicts. Occasionally their real feelings emerge, when they are caught off guard:

> Carol earns more than I do, but it doesn't usually cause any problems. Except it sometimes comes out in the heat of the moment. Like she might say, 'Why don't you give up your job and get a proper job? It's me that earns the money anyway'. We all get irrational in the heat of the moment. (Engineer, male)

ADVANTAGES OF AN EGALITARIAN DUAL-CAREER MARRIAGE

Couples who overcome the initial problems created by gender stereotypes and expectations forge a relationship based on friendship and equality. Partners do not need each other for total financial or domestic support, so they are not trapped in a cycle of mutual dependence. Those who stay together, working out a successful 'contract', do so because they benefit from each other's company, rather than needing a husband or wife in the traditional sense. A dual-career marriage provides opportunities for personal growth and the potential for overall happiness is greater than in conventional marriages.[18]

The sharing of the provider role also has substantial advantages to couples who resolve their ambivalence about not conforming to traditional roles. Marital satisfaction tends to be higher in families with a higher income, but this rule often fails to apply when the money is earned mainly by the wife.[19] Couples who feel comfortable with the wife's equal or superior earning capacity can enjoy a higher income without feeling threatened. Increasingly, husbands are recognising the benefits of not being the sole – or even the major – provider. They can reduce their work involvement during the childrearing years if they wish (although corporate leaders are not always happy with this decision), and a second income can cushion the effect of a career change. Career opportunities may be constrained, but, in some cases, opportunities may be expanded:

> We couldn't live off my income at the moment. If Barbara wasn't earning as much as she does, I would have had to carry on teaching instead of being able to branch out on my own. (Father of two, embarking on a new business)

Dual-career couples also benefit from a sense of colleagueship, shared interests and often shared expertise – which all strengthen the marital bond:

> We work in very similar environments. I work with people in a similar field to Susan and she occasionally works with merchant bankers. We even have some clients in common. We have professional engagements where either or both of us would be invited in our own right, but not together. On one occasion we were even introduced to each other. So we have complementary interests. (Banker, male)

Problems may arise if partners lack the time and energy to provide the practical or emotional support associated with a homemaker wife. The other side of the coin, however, is that spouses who spend their time engaged in similar activities have a better understanding of each other's work experiences. Social support is an important factor buffering the impact of stressful experiences.[20] However, Suzanne Kobasa has pointed out that there are different types of social support.[21] A person trying to cope with a stressful experience, such as being passed over for promotion, might look to other people for support in the form of sympathy. Alternatively, they may seek out someone who can talk over this problem, helping them to see why a situation has occurred and what constructive steps should be taken in the future. The latter type of support is more effective in dealing with stress. It is also the type of support which dual-career spouses are often able to offer each other:

> There are times when we both come home like bears with sore heads. The business contacts wouldn't see it, but the children do. But there are a lot of pluses. I can come home and discuss a problem and he'll understand and vice versa. I'm not sure how those families where spouses don't know about each other's professions cope. (Chartered Accountant, female)

In extolling the virtues of shared experiences, a favourable comparison is often made with what a traditional relationship might be like:

> I think a married couple have less opportunity to understand each other if one person is at home all day. They don't share common experiences. Its just as difficult for the one who's been out all day to recognise the problems of the person who is at home, as it is the other way around. (Manager, female)

MEN AND WOMEN IN ORGANISATIONS

Studies of female and male managers have suggested that some men find it difficult to relate to women as colleagues and equals, and especially to accept a woman boss.[22] These men feel more confident relating to women in line with their conditioned expectations; as mother figures, secretaries, lovers or (traditional, supportive) wives. As more dual-career marriages evolve as real partnerships of equals, and as the more successful wife with supportive husband gradually becomes as acceptable as the reverse pattern, relationships at work will also change. This will lead to more effective communication and greater co-operation. Meanwhile, as we have seen, we live in a transitional period in which most dual-earner couples strive for parity in their relationship, but struggle with traditional gender stereotypes and expectations. These dilemmas also continue to be reflected in the workplace.

Gender stereotypes determine the ways in which members of each sex are expected to behave and the ways in which their behaviour is interpreted. Men are expected to be competitive, rational and independent, women to be nurturant, emotional and dependent.[23] Stereotypes obscure real individual differences. Often they become self-fulfilling, as when a woman is not expected to be capable of a particular job, and is therefore given inadequate training and support.

As men's and women's roles change, stereotypes may eventually be modified – meanwhile, others develop. An example of a new stereotype is that of women who use the title Ms. There is evidence that women using this title are judged to be high on 'masculine' characteristics, such as competence, achievement orientation, independence and boastfulness and also low on traditional 'feminine' characteristics, such as dependence, expressiveness and warmth.[24] As with most stereotypes, this has evolved from the observation of some actual differences. More career women than housewives prefer this form of address.[25] However, it has been extended inappropriately, to obscure the many individual differences among women who pursue careers.

Different worlds, different styles

While gender stereotypes are over-inclusive and pernicious, there is much evidence that gender differences in style of communication and relating to others, do exist.[26] These differences are rooted in childhood experiences. There are marked differences in the ways in which people talk to girls and boys, and in what each sex is permitted to say and do, which shape their experiences as they grow up. Boys tend to play games which have winners and losers in large, hierarchical groups. They frequently boast and jostle for position. They learn to interact in terms of status. Girls tend to play in pairs or small groups, and to have a best friend. They are not encouraged to boast. Giving orders, which is acceptable for boys, is regarded as 'bossy'. Above all, girls, and later women, tend to emphasise connectedness rather than status.

Deborah Tannen argues, in her book *You Just Don't Understand*, that men and women inhabit different worlds.[27] They represent different cultures and speak different languages. As most people assume that others share their reality, they also tend to interpret others' communication in terms of their own style, emphasising connectedness or status. Tannen provides numerous examples of how different messages are interpreted differently by men and women, often causing conflict or resentment. For example, if someone says that they must check with their spouse before making an arrangement, this tends to be viewed negatively by men, positively by women. Men emphasise status and independence, and may interpret this need to consult a partner as being controlled or overly dependent. Women tend to emphasise connectedness and to see this action as demonstrating closeness or consideration for others' needs.

The different languages used by men and women can block effective communication. This is not to say that one form of communication or relating to others in superior. Male styles of relating and communicating are typically valued by organisations, although so-called 'feminine' characteristics such as concern for others, power-sharing and supportiveness are increasingly valued as managerial strengths. Rather than one form of relating to others being the norm, it is important to identify and understand these differences in order to accommodate diversity. Organisations need people who can both co-operate and compete.

HOW GENDER STEREOTYPES CAUSE MISUNDERSTANDINGS AT WORK

Interviews with men and women attending management development sessions revealed a number of issues in male-female interactions at work, arising from gender stereotypes and from the different perspectives of the two sexes. These often led to misunderstandings, discomfort or poor performance. Two areas were particularly damaging: notions of women as the weaker sex, and of women as sex objects.

Women as 'the weaker sex'

The notion that women are the weaker sex has long been used to 'protect' women against the rigours of certain types of work. Protective legislation was first introduced in this country in the 19th century. It was valuable in that it protected women against certain types of exploitation, but at the same time it placed women in the same category as children, and reinforced their dependence on men. Most protective legislation is now irrelevant. However, some men, influenced by traditional assumptions, still feel it necessary to protect women, whom they, perhaps unconsciously, see as weaker and less able to stand up to the rigours of the world of work. Older men, in particular, may adopt a fatherly attitude to younger women, rushing to their assistance or screening them from difficult situations. This can reduce women's opportunities to learn and develop. The reluctance to let women face the real world is illustrated by a male manager's difficulties with a female graduate trainee:

> I am actually giving her, probably, an inadequate amount of work to do, and extending her training beyond what is necessary ... I'd have done the same with a man, but if I'm honest with myself I've done it perhaps a little more, because she's a woman, for protection against the real world, sort of thing ... Because she's a woman, she needs that extra credibility. Perhaps that's why I want her to win her first few battles.

Most women feel patronised and frustrated by such an approach, which puts them on an unequal footing with men at the same stage in their careers. Nevertheless, some women, perhaps because of years of conditioning, collude with the notion of their vulnerability. This, of course, reinforces male paternalistic behaviours.

> I can often get my own way better than a man. I suppose I ask them to do me a favour. I sort of imply that I need it because I'm a woman, weaker, more needy.

Despite playing along with the stereotype of women as the weaker sex, the woman manager quoted above was aware of the damage she was doing;

> The other side of the coin is, I think, that they (men) don't take me as seriously as they would a man, in other situations.

Protection of women at work by a well-meaning, but misguided, chivalry by men can thus restrict women's opportunities to develop and succeed, while collusion by women can restrict their credibility and authority.

We also found evidence of a reluctance among some men to criticise or confront female staff. This stems partly from the desire to protect women, but also from stereotyped notions of how women will react.

> It's difficult to criticise a woman member of staff. She might

burst into tears. It scares me to death, the thought of a woman in tears in the office.

Again, some women may collude with this image, but it is a self-handicapping response. Feedback, both negative and positive, is essential for people to learn and develop, so lack of criticism is ultimately harmful. What often happens is that unspoken criticisms accumulate over time and eventually the woman is confronted with a situation that is much more difficult to handle than constructive comments at the appropriate time. This can then be upsetting, and so the belief that women cannot handle criticism becomes self-fulfilling. This process is illustrated by a female personnel officer:

I thought everything was going fine. Then I went for my appraisal review and I was told that I come over as really insensitive. My boss said everybody said that about me. I was devastated. He had never said anything to me before, nor had anybody else. It seemed like they had all been talking about me behind my back. I couldn't say anything. I was really upset.

SEXUALITY AND SEXUAL HARASSMENT

Barbara Gutek, author of *Sex and the Workplace*, argues that most of the social rules we use concerning male and female interaction have been formulated for social sexual behaviour.[28] These rules are therefore inappropriate for guiding relationships in the workplace. Nevertheless, they frequently do just that, because of a process which Gutek terms *sex role spillover*. This describes the spillover of gender stereotypes into the workplace, where women are expected to demonstrate the qualities associated with traditional female roles.

One of the characteristics assumed to be associated with femaleness is being a sex object. Research into prevalent beliefs about maleness and femaleness shows that the female stereotype includes characteristics such as sexiness and attractiveness, while there is no strongly held comparable belief about man. Rather, the stereotype of maleness centres around competence and activity.[29] Gutek argues that working women are, therefore, often defined as sex objects by colleagues and superiors, regardless of their own actions. Furthermore, women are often trivialised for their assumed sexuality and seductiveness in the workplace or, if they take steps to avoid being classed as a sex object, given

pejorative labels, such as prude, old maid or (used in a deroga-
tory way) lesbian.[30] By contrast, men who are overtly sexual in
the workplace are often accepted, and even given relatively
positive labels, such as 'a bit of a lady's man'. Gutek argues that
even if men behave in a way which is clearly detrimental to the
organisation, such as hiring the wrong women for the wrong
reasons, this tends to be regarded as a personal proclivity rather
than as work behaviour. Thus because there is no strongly
recognised sexual component to the male gender role, men's
inappropriate sexual behaviour tends to go unnoticed.

These stereotypes can have adverse consequences, particularly
for women at work, and ultimately for corporate health and
effectiveness. One consequence of the emphasis on women as
primarily sex objects may be the avoidance of otherwise desirable
working arrangements, such as business trips, office arrangements or informal business activities.

> If I have to go on a business trip, I would automatically take
> my assistant with me, but it does raise a problem with her
> being a woman. It's not that anything untoward would
> happen if we stayed in the same hotel, but I'm conscious that
> tongues would wag.

This dilemma illustrates the lack of 'rules' available for non-
sexual colleague relationships between men and women. Problems will flourish in an overtly sexualised workforce, such as
one in which posters of naked women or sexualised jokes are
accepted, and in any culture which emphasises sexuality rather
than professionalism.

Lack of professionalism and the treatment of women as sex
objects also enable sexual harassment to take place. Sexual harassment is any unwanted sexual attention and involves, for the
most part, men harassing women. Harassment of an employee
constitutes less favourable treatment on the grounds of sex, and
can amount to unlawful sex discrimination. The motives of the
harasser, who may claim he intended to flatter, are irrelevant.
Aside from the legal implications of tolerating sexual harassment
within the organisation, there are also human resource implications. Women who are harassed at work oftem suffer low self-
esteem and psychological distress,[31] and work performance may
suffer. High turnover of women staff will also occur in such an
environment.

It is important to recognise that sexual harassment is an
organisational, and not a personal problem. It is only a problem

in organisations which permit, or even encourage, an unprofes-
sional, sexual ethos, and fail to take allegations of sexual harassment seriously.

WHAT CAN ORGANISATIONS DO?

Ensure equal opportunities at work and at home

We have seen that there is a close link between dilemmas in dual-
earner partner relationships and dilemmas of male-female relationships in the workplace. Family inequality in domestic work,
and discomfort with non-traditional patterns of relative income,
stem from ambivalence about gender expectations. This
ambivalence and inequality is reflected in difficulties in the
workplace. These arise because men and women react to gendered categories, rather than as individuals. Enhanced communication and de-gendered interaction between spouses, will thus
ultimately benefit the organisation. Employers can assist dual-
earner families in their struggle towards new kinds of relationships, by introducing family friendly policies (see Chapter 8), and
by encouraging men as well as women to take advantage of
these, without fear of jeopardising their careers. Inequalities in
the family are also reinforced by the gender gap in earnings.
Organisations can lead the way to social as well as corporate
change by ensuring the appropriateness and effectiveness of their
equal opportunities policies (see Chapter 9).

Gender awareness training

Some companies, including, for example, British Rail, have
introduced gender awareness training to help staff to explore
their beliefs about the characteristics of women and men, and the
effects that these beliefs have on themselves and on the organisation. Typically, gender awareness sessions take the form of
single sex workshops, followed by mixed sex workshops, and
finally a return to single sex groups. In initial single sex groups,
participants look at how they became the men or women that
they are and the major influences on their lives. They also prepare for what they want to say to the other sex in the safe
environment of the mixed gender awareness groups. Here, men
and women listen to each other talk about what it means to them
to be a man or a woman, and the changes they would like the
other sex to make. Women speak first to break conventional
patterns, and no interruptions are permitted. Often members of

each sex are asked to repeat what members of the other sex are saying, until they get it right. This is a powerful means of helping men and women to overcome differences in communication style and to listen to one another. Finally, participants return to single sex groups to discuss what they have learnt in the mixed groups, and to explore joint action plans.

Other forms of training

Assertiveness training is discussed in relation to work and family issues in Chapter 7. Assertive skills are also useful in overcoming some of the communication problems discussed in this chapter. For example, men who are uncomfortable about criticising or confronting women may benefit from learning to give criticism assertively, rather than aggressively or not at all. This involves: criticising specific behaviours rather than the actual person, owning one's feelings, and never repeating other people's criticisms of the person, and offering constructive suggestions. For example, 'It seems to me that you didn't take Tom's workload into consideration when you set that deadline. Would it be better if you did it this way?' is preferable to 'You are an insensitive person. Everyone says so'. Men may also find it easier to confront women if women respond to criticism in an assertive way, that is: accepting valid criticisms and learning from them; denying invalid criticisms and asking for more information about why the criticism has been made; and refusing to take 'put downs'. Of course, both men and women need both these types of skills. The point is that assertive behaviour can help those people who are reacting to, or colluding with stereotypes, to overcome them.

Discourage sexual harassment

Ensure that there is an effective policy on sexual harassment. This should set out clear guidelines about the sorts of behaviour which are unacceptable in the workplace. It should also include a clear set of procedures for dealing with complaints. It is important to ensure that all complaints are taken seriously, and that complainants are not punished in any way, so that victims can feel comfortable in coming forward. Where there is evidence of harassment, action should be taken against the perpetrators. This is essential to reinforce the message that such behaviour is unacceptable. Guidelines on policy concerning sexual harassment are available from the Equal Opportunities Commission and the Department of Employment.

Promote professional behaviour and ambience throughout the organisation

This may involve tackling the 'macho' ethos in many departments. Clearly, this will be difficult in many traditionally male-dominated environments. The alternative, however, is to perpetuate working environments in which it is difficult for women to feel comfortable. This may make it impossible to recruit the best people for certain jobs.

Of course, men and women are increasingly meeting in the workplace, and serious relationships will sometimes develop between them. In the interest of professionalism, however, there should be guidelines on what is acceptable behaviour *at work*. In this respect, work and home life should be kept separate.

REFERENCES

1. Henwood, M, Rimmer, L and Wicks, M (1987) *Inside the Family: Changing Roles of Men and Women*, London: Family Policies Study Centre.
2. Gilbert, L A and Dancer, L S (1992) 'Dual Earner Families in the United States and Effects on Adolescents', in S Lewis, D N Izraeli and H Hootsmans (eds), *Dual Earner Families, International Perspectives*, London: Sage.
3. Brannen, J and Moss, P (1991) *Managing Mothers: Dual Earner Households After Maternity Leave*, London: Unwin Hyman.
4. Rapoport, R and Rapoport, R N (1976) *Dual Career families Re-examined*, New York: Harper and Row.
5. Pleck, J H (1985) *Working Wives/Working Husbands*, Beverly Hills, California: Sage.
6. Rapoport, R and Rapoport, R N (1976) op cit.
7. Gilbert, L A (1985) *Men in Dual Career Families*, Hillsdale, NJ; Lawrence Erlbaum.
8. Cook, A H (1992) 'Can work requirements accommodate to meet the needs of dual earner families?' in S Lewis, D N Izraeli and H Hootsmans (eds) op cit.
9. Izraeli, D N (1989) 'Burning out in medicine', in E B Goldsmith (ed), *Work and Family. Theory, Research and Applications*, Newbury Park, California: Sage.
10. Pleck, J H (1985) op cit.
11. Brannen, J and Moss, P (1987) 'Dual earner households: Women's financial contributions after the birth of the first

child', in J Brannen and G Wilson (eds), *Give and Take in Families*, Unwin Hyman, London.

12. Ferree, M M (1987) 'The struggles of superwoman', in C Bose, K Feldberg and N Sokoloff, (eds), *Hidden Aspects of Women's Work*, New York: Praeger.
13. Brannen, J and Moss, P (1991) op cit.
14. Hiller, D V and Philliber, W W (1982) 'Predicting marital and career success among dual career couples', *Journal of Marriage and the Family*, 53–62.
15. Lewis, S and Cooper, C L (1987) 'Stress in dual earner couples and stage in the life cycle', *Journal of Occupational Psychology*, 60, 289–303.
16. Lewis, S and Cooper, C L (1987) ibid.
17. Berman, E, Sachs, S and Lief, H (1975) 'The two professional marriage. A new conflict syndrome', *Journal of Sex and Marital Therapy*, 1, 242–253.
18. Benin, M H and Nienstedt, B C (1985) 'Happiness in dual and single earner families. The effects of marital happiness, job satisfaction and stage in the life cycle', *Journal of Marriage and the Family*, 975–982.
19. Betz, N and Fitzgerald, L (1987) *The Career Psychology of Women*, New York: Academic Press.
20. Williams, D R and House, J S (1985) 'Social support and stress reduction', in C L Cooper and M J Smith (eds), *Job Stress and Blue Collar Work*, London: Wiley.
21. Kobasa, S and Puccetti, M (1983) 'Personality and social resources in stress resistance', *Journal of Personality and Social Psychology*, 45, 4, 834–850.
22. Kanter, R M (1977) *Men and Women of the Organization*, New York: Basic Books.
23. Williams, J E and Best, D L (1982) *Measuring Sex Stereotypes, A Thirty Nation Study*, Beverley Hills, California: Sage.
24. Dion, L K and Cota, A A (1991) 'The Ms stereotypes. Its domain and the role of explicitness in title preference', *Pscychology of Women Quarterly*, 15, 403–410.
25. Dion, L K and Cota, A A ibid.
26. Tannen, D (1992) *You Just Don't Understand*, Virago, London.
27. Tannen, D (1992) ibid.
28. Gutek, B A (1985) *Sex and the Workplace. Impact of Sexual Behaviour, and Harassment on Women, Men and Organizations*, San Francisco, California: Jossey-Bass.
29. Williams, J E and Best, D L (1982) op cit.
30. Gutek, B A (1989) 'Sexuality in the workplace; Key issues in

social research and organisational practice', in Hearn, J, Sheppard, D L, Tancred-Sheri, P and Burrell, G, *The Sexuality of Organizations*, London: Sage.

31.   Gutek, B A (1985) op cit.

7

Looking at Alternatives

The workaholic way of life demanded by many firms seriously diminishes personal and domestic life, often leading to divorce.[1] An egalitarian dual-career relationship is unlikely to be a realistic goal for men working under this sort of pressure, while women often feel that they are forced to choose between having a successful career and a family:

> If I want to get on, I have to be seen to be in the office from 8 in the morning until 8 at night. I am ambitious, but at some stage I would like to have children. Eventually I am just going to have to make difficult choices. (Financial Adviser, female)

Apart from the adverse personal effects of excessive work, several of the participants in our study questioned the value of long hours in terms of productivity and efficiency. Losing contact with the community can be a further disadvantage in many occupations.

Many people work long hours, not because this is necessary from the point of view of productivity, but to compete with their peers. Total involvement in work to the exclusion of all other aspects of life, together with competitiveness and the inevitable hostility with which it is often associated, may sound familiar. This closely resembles the Type A coronary-prone behaviour pattern (see Chapter 2). This type of behaviour needs actively to be discouraged for the sake of the health of the workforce. Furthermore, competitive behaviour at work can cause job dissatisfaction, and may result in lower, overall productivity.[2]

Organisations need to ask themselves the following questions:

- Do employees need to work more than a 35-hour week? If so, why? At the turn of the century, a 60-hour week was usual. Perhaps we should now be re-evaluating the desirability of a 35-hour plus week.

- What is the impact of excessive working hours on employees' family life?
- What is the impact on employees' personal health?
- Does the organisation really benefit in the long term from long working hours?

ALTERNATIVE WORKING ARRANGEMENTS

A range of flexible working arrangements can be introduced to increase employees' control over the hours they work, which would benefit the dual-earner couple. When individuals are able to choose the style of work which suits them, they will be less stressed. As a result, they are better able to concentrate and perform at work, with less worry about what is happening at home. Rigid, inflexible working hours are particularly stressful and inappropriate for parents of young children. In fact, most of the participants in our study, whether or not they were parents, wanted more flexibility in their working lives.

Flexitime

Flexitime is a system which permits variable times of arrival and departure within limits set by management. A standard number of hours have to be worked during a given time, but the exact time can be flexible. There is usually, but not always, a core period during which everyone must work. This system does not create more time for family and home life, but provides individuals with more control, enabling them to balance all the demands in their lives. Flexitime is of great assistance to parents who need to co-ordinate their working hours with the schedules of schools and nurseries, with medical appointments and with other obligations. However, to see flexitime as necessary only for working parents is to marginalise its importance. Flexitime has benefits for all employees, which include making shopping and other activities easier and alleviating rush-hour traffic problems. It can also be used by employees to pursue further education, as well as help those who are recovering from illness or preparing for retirement.

Flexitime, however, is not the perfect solution. It can be extremely effective in reducing the stress of combining work and family, when both partners have the benefit of a flexitime system, and when spouses have non-traditional sex roles.[3] However, in more traditional families, where the assumption is that the woman is responsible for domestic work and childcare, flexitime can enable female employees to fit in more family activities without increasing the contribution of their husbands.[4] Both men and women need to be encouraged to use flexitime to accommodate their family schedules.

The benefits of flexitime vary according to the system in use. Sheila Kamerman and Alfred Khan describe four different types of flexitime in the USA, from the least to the most flexible.[5]

- *Flexitour.* Employees choose their starting and ending times, but must keep within the schedule they select and work the same number of hours each day.
- *Glidingtime.* This is similar to flexitour, except that employees may vary the time they start and finish each day.
- *Variable day.* Employees can vary the number of hours worked each day, providing they are present for a minimum core period.
- *Maxiflex.* Daily hours can be varied as desired. Employees are not required to be present for any core period.

Systems that allow maximum flexibility permit employees to opt to work a compressed work week. This involves working for ten or more hours a day for three or four working days. One choice could be an extended weekend, which would benefit commuting couples. It can also be used by both parents of young children to enable them to share childcare.

A particularly innovative form of flexible working is the flexible working year. This has proved to be successful in several firms in the formal West Germany, although the idea has not been widely implemented elsewhere.[6] Employees' net working hours are decided for a whole year and individuals are free to choose their own working times as to fulfil the yearly quota. This has advantages for both the employee and the organisation. The employee is provided with the flexibility to work longer hours at certain periods and reduce working during, for example, school holidays, while continuing to retain a secure and regular system of payment. Payment is by means of a monthly salary, regardless of the number of hours worked during that period. The benefits to employers will depend upon the nature of the organisation.

The German experience suggests that these benefits may include improved ability to handle seasonal or cyclical fluctuations because of a more flexible workforce. The firm is able to take full advantage of a vast pool of full-time, part-time, job sharing and even seasonal staff. 'Flexiyear' is used as an umbrella term for all these different categories. Employees have the opportunity to work less than 40 hours a week without losing their full-time status, while temporary or seasonal staff enjoy a change of status by becoming permanent employees. Finally, by fitting working time to people's needs, there is greater productivity and lower absenteeism and turnover.

Companies which have not yet implemented a flexitime system should consider doing so. Others can review the adequacy of their system in the light of the needs of employees and of the organisation. Employees' needs should be assessed, possibly through a company-wide survey, to determine which system would be most valuable. Once implemented, flexible working arrangements should be monitored to ensure that they are fulfilling needs and are available to the whole workforce. One woman we interviewed noted that the flexitime system operated by her organisation was irrelevant to her, as she was expected to be at work during the same hours as her boss. It is essential that flexitime is introduced as a means of providing employees with genuine control over the hours they work, and not as a token gesture.

Research in Denmark suggests that both men and women work longer than they need to if they can work flexibly,[7] a finding which has led some commentators to suggest that this could, in some cases, create its own stress. This is more likely to happen when family needs are not recognised.

In many companies, flexibility is negotiated informally between colleagues, or between managers and staff. The extent to which this is negotiated around family responsibilities tends to vary according to whether there are more male or female staff. For example, children tend to be more visible in female-dominated organisations, while one study found that in a male-dominated police station, family reasons were sufficient for a weekend off. The demands of an extra job, however, gave immediate entitlement to time off.

Flexiplace

Helpful companies can be flexible about where, as well as when, employees work. Employees may be able to work at home or spread their workload between home and the office or workplace. Many types of work are amenable to flexiplace, including editing, accounting, designing and computer programming. The limits to flexible locations are set by the need for contact with clients, patients or others and the need for specific equipment which is only available at the workplace. In some cases, clients may be prepared to visit a person's home rather than a central workplace. Clearly, there are some times when the transfer of equipment, such as a laboratory, to the home is not practical. Nevertheless, technological advances mean that an increasing amount of equipment can be used in alternative locations. Information technology, including personal computers, data bases and fax systems, makes *telecommuting*, whereby employees work off-site linked to a central office by a computer, increasingly feasible. According to some predictions, the need for a central workplace is set to decrease dramatically.[8]

In part, the growth of telecommunicating has been in response to the need to retain the skills and expertise of experienced staff, especially women who have taken maternity leave. Working from home enables mothers or fathers of young children, as well as employees with responsibilities for elderly relatives, to continue to combine their career with family commitments. It is also of benefit to spouses who work in different locations and is a possible solution to relocation problems. For instance, Jane, an area sales manager for a computer company in the south of England, is able to spend at least two or three working days a week telecommunicating and staying in her home in the north, where her husband is a recruitment consultant.

ICL offer opportunities for off-site employment for trained computer personnel, who cannot or do not wish to undertake conventional full-time employment. In 1990, there were approximately 350 off-site employees. Hours are flexible, but employees contract to be available for a specified minimum number. Remuneration is at an hourly rate, calculated on the basis of the appropriate full-time annual salary. Off-site workers are graded, appraised and reviewed on the same terms as on-site staff, and are entitled to the same benefits, on a pro rata basis. This enables parents (mostly mothers) to continue in interesting, worthwhile employment, and to return to full-time employment without having lost touch with the rapidly developing computer industry.

The instigation of homeworking involves investment in home computers and other equipment, but can be cost-effective in the long term. Apart from saving the expense of training new staff, the spread of telecommuting will ultimately reduce investment in office space and increase efficiency by reducing commuting time. It may also have a positive impact on pollution and the environment.

A dispersed workforce calls for new managerial skills.

Homeworkers may feel isolated and cease to see themselves as members of the larger organisation. It is essential that this is countered by regular meetings, and possibly by the arrangement of social events. The experience of telecommuting at Control Data suggests that success depends on manager-employee relations, with management the greatest obstacle.[9] Some managers persist in believing that they cannot trust people whom they cannot see. Often they fear losing control and power because of the lack of visible employees. The solution lies in education, whereby managers will realise that they will be able to supervise more people more efficiently, while at the same time responding to employees' family needs.

REDUCING WORKING HOURS

Part-time work

Part-time working tends to be limited to relatively low status jobs, with restricted benefits and limited access to training and opportunities for promotion. Organisations need to question the assumption that only employees who work full-time are serious about their careers. A period of transition involving part-time work is desirable for new parents. It is guaranteed for both mothers and fathers in Sweden. When both spouses are employed, one or both can afford to work part-time hours when their children are young or while they have other family commitments. However, highly trained individuals are unlikely to be satisfied in dead-end jobs in which their skills are under-utilised. What is needed are part-time jobs with career opportunities, which take account of employees' family and professional needs.

Some of the professions are now recognising the need to upgrade part-time opportunities, to avoid losing the skills of their female members. Within the health service, part-time training opportunities are available in all specialties, for doctors and dentists with domestic commitments, or for those who are disabled. Although opportunities are limited, it is possible to become a consultant through a part-time route. The Law Society's report of the 'Working Party on Women's Careers',[10] emphasises that part-time employees should be seen as a flexible and valuable resource, and not as 'second best'. Neither should part-time work be restricted to employees. The Working Party advocates the setting up of part-time partnerships, with a pro rata share of the profits. Providing that the situation is explained to clients, they should have no difficulty in accepting this. One female solicitor explained that clients usually telephone in the morning, which is when she is available. A legal secretary can deal with calls at other times or refer clients to the solicitor's home if he or she is working on split locations. A potential problem of a part-time partnership can be the difficulties in sharing office administration, but this can be reflected in the share of profits. The Law Society suggests a further model of part-time working, which is that of the freelance consultant who is paid according to the work undertaken. Part-time employment, training and partnerships could benefit women and men in a range of occupations, and some large companies, including retail chains and banks, are beginning to offer part-time jobs with pro rata benefits and career opportunities.

Job sharing

If attendance on a full-time basis is essential, companies can consider offering job-share opportunities. The popularity of job sharing is growing for positions in management and elsewhere, in local authorities, banks, retail chain stores, firms of solicitors and a number of other types of organisations. Employers see the advantages in terms of retaining skilled and experienced staff. It is also recognised that working part-time allows people to stay fresh, energetic and creative during the hours worked, and there is evidence of greater productivity among job sharers.[11]

V-time

V-time or *voluntary reduced time* is a system which allows full-time employees to reduce working hours for a specified period, with a concomitant reduction in salary.[12] It differs from the usual concept of part-time work in that it is temporary, with a guaranteed opportunity to return to full-time. Usually, the schedule remains in force for a designated period, perhaps six or 12 months, to allow employees and employers to try the new arrangements, with the assurance that the commitment can be renegotiated or terminated after this period. All employee benefits are maintained during the period of reduced work, which may be on a regular basis, such as shorter days or weeks, or may be a block of time, perhaps taken during school holidays. V-time is another useful strategy to create opportunities to balance work with other responsibilities, and may also be used by employees for gaining new skills or responding to a health problem.

Sabbaticals

Sabbaticals also create similar opportunities. In Sweden, the idea of a year or less off, after a certain period of work, has been institutionalised in a wide range of occupations. In the UK six-month sabbaticals for employees aged 50 or over with at least 25 years' service have been introduced by the John Lewis group to allow employees to do things they enjoy which would not otherwise be possible.[13] Sabbaticals are available at all levels, and those in specialist and senior management posts are encouraged not to feel indispensable, although they are required to give longer notice than other employees. Arrangements are made to cover their absences by creating an opportunity for a trainee, or reorganising colleagues' responsibilities to share out the work. This provides other employees with the opportunities to take on a higher level of responsibility, which may contribute to personal and career development. It appears that colleagues are willing to co-operate, knowing that they, too, will have the opportunity of a sabbatical. The restriction to those aged over 50 makes this initiative of little use to new parents, but sabbaticals may be used for other family obligations. Apart from the care of sick relatives, people might wish to spend the time visiting adult children living abroad. Finally, the fact that the system works successfully has implications for the organisation of leave of absence for younger employees, especially for those taking maternity or parental leave.

EASING THE TRANSITION TO PARENTHOOD

In Chapter 4, we discussed the problems associated with the transition to parenthood for dual-career couples. There are several innovative ways in which responsive organisations can, and do, help to make life easier for new parents. The alternative work schedules described above, in particular some form of reduced hours, are often welcomed during a period of transition, by parents coping with disturbed nights or breastfeeding. Some firms offer other benefits and concessions above the legal minimum. These include extended leave or financial benefits beyond the statutory maternity allowance. At the very least, organisations should ease the financial burden of maternity leave by covering job-related items, such as membership fees for professional bodies and car expenses. Paid maternity leave is a benefit which is particularly effective in attracting and retaining high-calibre female applicants.

Network groups, comprising women who have experienced maternity leave, exist in several companies. Such groups offer advice and support for those away from work and also for returners. Workshops and seminars held during the firm's time, or in the lunch-hour, can help new parents deal with issues ranging from feelings of guilt to childcare problems. As women returning from leave sometimes take a while to settle back into their routine, refresher courses can help them to re-integrate more easily. Above all, however, women value evidence that decisions on promotion are made without regard to their family obligations.

Women who are self-employed, such as principals in medical practice or partners in firms of accountants, solicitors or architects, are not covered by legislation, and are therefore expected to make their own provision for maternity leave. A maternity clause could be automatically included in partnership deeds, so that women are not put in the position of having to raise and negotiate the issue at a time when they might feel it would prejudice their chances of admission to the partnership.

The question of time off for fathers for childcare is not yet a pressing issue for most men in the UK. There is still the perception that women are the primary parents. Nevertheless, some fathers in dual-career marriages would welcome the opportunity to be more involved in looking after their children. Paternity leave in various forms does exist to some extent in the UK, although it is usually brief and not always paid. Other men still suffer penalities, such as employer hostility, loss of pay or, in the extreme, job loss, if they take time off work around the time of childbirth.[14] Better provisions for paid paternity leave would be of potential benefit to women and men, and to children, who would be able to form a closer bond with both parents. Parental leave, which is discussed in Chapter 9, is another way of enabling both parents to be involved in childcare, while retaining continuity in their careers.

Career break schemes

Currently, less than 7 per cent of women in the UK return to full-time work after maternity leave, whereas 90 per cent return after a longer break.[15] Maternity or paternity leave is not suitable for all parents, many of whom prefer to spend longer with their infants. Realising that breaks for childcare are usually temporary, some organisations have taken steps to accommodate a longer career break. Re-entry and retainer schemes have been initiated to allow some employees to interrupt their usual working arrangements for a number of years, after which they can return to the organisations with no loss of seniority.[16] Career breaks are open, in principle, to both men and women, although they tend to be taken only by women. Organizations which allow two short career breaks could encourage the sharing of these between the two parents. The employee is usually expected to undertake at least two weeks' paid relief work for the organisation during each year of her absence and is provided with regular information packs, as well as a refresher course on her return. In practice, many participants work for more than two weeks a year during their career break. The scheme may permit one five-year break or two shorter breaks, each commencing from the end of statutory maternity leave. Many women prefer two shorter breaks, which enables them to return to work between the births of their children. Ideally, the choice of one long or two short breaks could be left to the employee.

The benefits of operating a career-break scheme are becoming increasingly apparent. For example:

- They ensure that participants remain in touch with their work, maintaining confidence and expertise.
- Firms operating these schemes will attract young women with talent and ambition, because of the reduced prospect of having to choose between family and career.
- They ensure that investment in training is not lost.
- They enable successful employment at a future date and with a minimum of retraining required.
- They provide role models of women who are successfully combining career and family.
- They improve motivation, timekeeping and productivity.
- They increase organisational flexibility by providing a pool of trained staff to draw on when people are absent or during peak periods.
- They avoid skill shortages, especially in industries where it is difficult to attract female employees.
- They reduce stress among new parents.
- They reduce costs incurred in advertisements and reinstatement due to loss of continuity of staff.

The career-break scheme first introduced by a major bank has served as a model for many forward-looking organisations and professional bodies who are now adopting similar schemes. The Law Society suggests that, in future, those operating such a scheme should ensure maximum benefit by advertising themselves as 'a career break employer', in much the same way as many organisations currently claim to be equal opportunity employers.

Assessing the needs of the workforce

The obvious benefits of alternative work patterns to organisations should not obscure the specific needs of individuals or groups of employees. Organisations need to consult with the workforce to see what they consider most helpful. One national firm of chartered accountants, for example, surveyed staff to determine the potential demand for career breaks. Responses indicated little demand for such schemes. Rather, professional staff favoured part-time or flexible work, to enable them to retain some involvement in work. Support staff also wanted to continue working, and felt that some form of childcare provision would be most helpful. An example of the questionnaire used can be found in the Appendix.

Finally, because both men and women have domestic responsibilities, both can benefit from policies which aim to ease the transition to parenthood and the management of work and family roles. Just as women need role models who are successfully combining career and motherhood, men require role models of fathers willing to accommodate childcare with their careers. Organisations have a role to play in bringing about the necessary change in attitudes by encouraging dual-career fathers who show an interest in paternity leave or career breaks. They can do this by sanctioning their choice and guaranteeing that there will be no damage to long-term career prospects. Ultimately, the most helpful organisations will be those that offer the widest choice and flexibility to new parents wanting to manage both career and parenthood in the way which suits their individual needs.

To ensure the effectiveness of policies introduced to enhance work and family opportunities, these should be regularly monitored and evaluated. Most evaluative research has tended to consider the views of managers, as well as focusing on cost effectiveness. Important though these perspectives are, employees, and perhaps their partners or other family members, also need to be consulted.[17]

REFERENCES

1. Lomas, C (1988) 'Factors associated with success', in *Women in Management: Optimising the Potential*, Ashridge Management College, Berkhamsted, Herts.
2. Bensahel, J (1978) 'Why competition may not always be healthy', *International Management*, 23, 5 (October).
3. Lee, R A (1983) 'Flexitime and conjugal roles', *Journal of Organizational Behavior*, 4, 297–315.
4. Bohen, B H and Viveros-Long, A (1981) *Balancing Jobs and Family Life: Do Flexible Work Schedules Help?* Temple University Press, Philadelphia.
5. Kamerman, S B and Khan, A J (1987) *The Responsive Workplace: Employers and a Changing Labor Force*, Columbia University Press, New York.
6. Teriet, B (1985) 'Flexible working years', in Clutterbuck, D (ed), *New Patterns of Work*, 98–194, Gower, Aldershot.
7. Huet, H, Thaulow, I and Maerkedahl, G (1992) *Do Working Time Arrangements Affect Stress and Welfare in the Family?*, paper presented at the National Council on Family Research Annual Conference, Orlando.
8. *Tomorrow's Workplace: Harnessing the Challenge of Teleworking* (1988) British Telecom and CBI, London.
9. Control Data Corporation (USA) (1985) 'Telecommuting', in Clutterbuck, D, op. cit., 127–136.
10. The Law Society (1988) 'Equal in the law', *Report of the Working Party on Women's Careers*, London.
11. Walton, P (1985) 'Job sharing', in Clutterbuck, D, op. cit., 110–127.
12. Moorman, B and Olmsted, B (1985) *V-time: A New Way to Work*, New Ways to Work, San Francisco.
13. May, S (1985) 'Sabbaticals: the John Lewis experience', in Clutterbuck, D, op. cit., 104–110.
14. Bell, C, McKee, L and Priestley, K (1983) *Fathers, Childbirth and Work*, Equal Opportunities Commission, Manchester.
15. Martin, J and Roberts, C (1984) *Women and Employment: A Lifetime Perspective*, Office of Population Censuses and Surveys, London.
16. Truman, C (1986) *Overcoming the Career Break: A Positive Approach*, UMIST, Manchester.
17. Lewis, S (forthcoming) 'Role conflict in dual-earner famil-

ies', in Davidson, M and Burke, D (eds) *Women in management: current research issues*, Paul Chapman, London.

8
Training and Development

In this chapter we discuss training and development, which can contribute towards meeting the needs of the new workforce at three levels:

- Management training to raise awareness of dual-career family issues.
- Training which anticipates work and family issues.
- Training in skills which help employees to manage current work and family commitments.

We look at each type of training, and also provide exercises which may be used as part of training or self-development programmes.

MANAGEMENT TRAINING

Many managers are only too aware of dual-earner family dilemmas, having struggled with them themselves. Too often, however, senior management consists primarily of men, the majority of whom have had non-career-orientated wives to shield them from family involvement. Consequently, companies such as Johnson and Johnson and IBM have introduced training programmes to encourage managers to become more sensitive to work and family issues. These programmes emphasise the business case for flexibility and review corporate policy and practice in the light of workforce needs.

Management training can take the form of workshops or seminars, in which case studies of dual-earner family issues, such as those described in earlier chapters of this book, are considered. Open discussion of the needs of dual-earner spouses and single parents will help to break the taboo against discussing domestic commitments. An important function of such exercises must be the exploration of organisational and personal prejudices. Executives can be encouraged to clarify their own values about the ideal career, parent and so on, and if not to change them, at least to value diversity, and consider how they can support the careers and lifestyles of younger members of their company. It is also important for senior management to consider the example they set as role models. Evidence suggests that healthy executives value their family time.[1] Those who model a workaholic style should, therefore, consider the impact of this on themselves as well as on younger members of their staff. This means acknowledging that productivity is not simply a function of number of hours worked.

It may be necessary, as part of management training and awareness raising, to explore why some managers are reluctant to consider family needs as relevant to a work context. This type of discussion can raise some painful issues. For example, some managers will have achieved career success by maximising their involvement with work and sacrificing other aspects of their lives. Sometimes this leads to marital conflict, divorce and/or difficult relationships with adolescent and adult children. Putting work/family issues on the agenda is, therefore, often resisted.

Management training is important for senior managers and those with the power to implement change. It is also essential for supervisors and first-line managers to be trained to be adaptable and responsive, as they are key figures in determining the success of formal work/family policies.

Our research suggests that many line managers in companies where family-orientated policies are being implemented would welcome training in the everyday management of staff who are benefiting from these provisions. For example, in a company with a reduced hours scheme for professionals, managers were unsure about how much to expect from someone on reduced hours when full-time hours tended to be much in excess of a normal working week. They also felt a need for guidance on how to appraise and set objectives for staff working reduced hours. At the very least, managers need an opportunity to discuss policies with colleagues. Family-oriented policies are a challenge for line managers, who may not previously have questioned the virtue of long hours of work, and need support to deal with this.

TRAINING WHICH ANTICIPATES WORK/FAMILY ISSUES

Training can encourage people to consider work/family issues before they arise. This may be accomplished in personal effectiveness and career/life planning courses. The aim is to enable employees at an early stage in their careers to consider their short- and long-term goals, to identify their strengths and resources towards achieving these ends, and also to identify any possible barriers as well as ways of overcoming them. It is increasingly acknowledged that for women this process must involve a consideration of their present and future family plans, which are intimately bound up with career issues. Both men and women need to consider career goals in the context of broader life goals.

Personal effectiveness training usually takes place in small, participative groups to facilitate a sharing of ideas and exploration of issues within a supportive context. The issues which arise often include (for example): if and when to have children; possible impact on careers; location and mobility issues; what happens if one person's career succeeds and not his or her partner's; unequal sharing of domestic work; and sex discrimination at work. Discussion can focus on identifying strategies for overcoming barriers. The value of open discussion of these issues is that:

- People realise that they are not alone in facing decisions and obstacles, and hence the personal becomes political.
- Anticipation of problems gives participants the opportunity to plan and take control of their lives. Individuals or couples can explore their own flexible way of managing their lives together, rather than responding to societal norms or company expectations.
- Various choices can be discussed and new and creative ideas explored such as commuter marriage (see Chapter 3) or role cycling. *Role cycling*[2] is a type of career and life planning used by some dual-career couples to ensure that intense work and family demands do not occur simultaneously, and that the maximum demands on each partner do not overlap. For instance, one partner may delay a particular activity such as studying for a further degree or seeking a promotion, until childcare demands or the spouse's work demands are diminished. Each partner will have the opportunity to do these things with the support of their spouse, but at different stages. This approach involves long-term planning and a willingness for both partners to be flexible and to accommodate the other. It may mean that opportunities cannot always be taken as and when they arise, and that certain

ambitions may have to be deferred. On the positive side, role cycling may be used to create opportunities for both partners at a time when it is convenient to them as a couple, avoiding overload on the way.

The following exercise might help an individual or couple to focus on work and family issues, now and in the future.

Exercise 1

Aim: To help participants to start to focus on life/career development issues.

Lifelines

1. Draw a *lifeline*, using any visual form (a line, circle etc.). You may prefer to draw two lines, for life and career, with intersections as relevant.
2. Mark where you are now. Indicate the most personally significant events in your life/career to date.
3. Indicate what you expect to be doing in the next x years (up to whatever age you choose). Indicate what you expect to be the significant events in the future, and when you would like them to occur.
4. Share these lifelines in pairs and perhaps in groups of four.

SKILLS FOR MANAGING WORK AND FAMILY

The objective of work/family management training is to help individuals reflect on actual and/or anticipated work/family issues and to identify and develop strategies for managing dual roles. There are three main components of such a programme: managing work/family conflict and overload; assertiveness skills for work /family management; and stress management.

Coping with conflict

Psychologists have identified three general approaches to coping with role conflict:

Type 1 coping: Changing other people's expectations
This is an attempt to alter other people's expectations of a par-

ticular role. For instance, a wife may renegotiate with her husband the expectation that she should be responsible for all domestic work, or an employee may negotiate with his or her boss about what should be expected in a particular job. Type 1 strategies include delegation and refusing to take on extra work (by being assertive).

Type 2 coping: Changing self-expectations
This is an attempt by an individual to change his or her own self-expectations and behaviours without necessarily trying to alter other people's attitudes. Making a personal decision to limit activities in the career, spouse or parental roles would be examples of Type 2 coping. Strategies include eliminating roles, such as giving up voluntary work or union activity, restricting social contacts and establishing priorities.

Type 3 coping: Role expansion – 'pleasing everyone'
Instead of attempting to change the situation or alter self-expectations, an individual may attempt to organise himself or herself in such a way that all role demands can be met. For instance, an overworked mother may work even harder to fit the superwoman image rather than delegating more domestic work to other family members, reducing work involvement, or lowering standards in the home. Strategies which enable individuals to do all this include planning, scheduling, working harder and denying that a situation is stressful.

Types 1 and 2 coping are both active coping orientations, in that they involve an attempt to change the situation in order to make it more manageable. Type 3 coping is more passive. It involves an acceptance of all demands made. Attempts are made to satisfy everyone's expectations by being more organised or by using techniques which will minimise the subsequent stress without eliminating or reducing its cause.

Research shows that role redefinition (changing our own or other people's expectations) tends to be more successful than role expansion strategies. Redefinition strategies produce higher levels of career satisfaction[3] and have been found to be more successful than role expansion in reducing conflicts between work and home.[4] Strategies involving the redefinition of roles are particularly effective in dealing with work-related problems[5] and with issues concerning relationships between spouses. However, traditional attitudes towards motherhood often make it difficult, even for women who articulate non-traditional beliefs, to alter their own or other people's expectations of the role of good mother.[6]

Exercise 2

Aim: To begin to identify your own approaches to coping with work/family conflict and to consider alternatives.

1. Draw a diagram depicting yourself (in any form, eg a circle or other symbol) and the people or institutions which make demands on your time. (For example, you might draw yourself as a circle and various other circles around you, representing spouse, children, parents, manager, colleagues etc.)
2. Identify the demands which are self-generated.
3. Identify which of these demands conflict with each other.
4. Discuss your diagram with a partner. Where do conflicting demands come from? Who or what are the greatest source of demands? To what extent are demands self-generated? What is the impact of social and organisational expectations?
5. Look at some of the conflicts identified in your diagram and consider the type of coping you generally use. Are they Type 1, 2 or 3? What are the pay-offs for the strategies? The costs? Would other strategies have greater pay-offs? Costs?

Recognising overload

Before steps can be taken to redefine expectations to reduce pressures, it is necessary to recognise that a problem exists. Overload, in particular, is often accepted as a fact of life and not defined as a problem. A study of 164 professional women conducted by Sarah Yogev in the USA revealed that mothers of young children worked a total of 107 hours a week or more in fulfilling their professional and parental duties.[7] Yet these women did not report feeling more overworked than childless women whose total hours were much shorter. Yogev explains these findings in terms of women's socialisation experiences. Most contemporary professional women were socialised initially into traditional attitudes towards the roles of wife and mother and may, therefore, evaluate their performance in family roles by comparing themselves with housewives. However, they have also been socialised into their professional roles, and evaluate their professional competence by comparing themselves with male colleagues. Subsequently, women take it for granted that having chosen to combine professional and family roles, they will have little time for themselves. Admitting to being overburdened appears to be an admission of inadequacy, implying that they are unable to integrate the two areas of their lives. For men, admitting that hours of work are too long or that the pressure is too great can also appear to be a sign of weakness due to their early conditioning, professional socialisation and the internalisation of the male work ethic.

Once it is recognised that the overload and conflict inherent in the dual-earner lifestyle are a consequence of conflicting expectations and not personal inadequacy, it should be possible to examine the sources of stress.

Exercise 3

Are you suffering from overload?

Consider whether any of the following statements apply to you. If so, it may be that you are suffering from overload and should consider steps to reduce your workload or to cope better with this situation.

I feel as though I am constantly under pressure

I am constantly tired

I feel that I have too much work to do in the time available

I find my work too difficult and have difficulty coping with it

There do not seem to be enough hours in the day to get everything done.

Exercise 4

To be completed prior to a course, retrospectively, or after a course, to reinforce the message.

Keep a diary for a typical week, noting how many hours are spent:

- in work-related activities
- in domestic work
- in childcare or other care
- travelling.

Add up your total hours for the week. If they are excessive and you have agreed with any of the statements in Exercise 3, ask yourself whether your combined workload really is inevitable.

Dealing with overload by establishing priorities

One way of managing multiple roles and avoiding overload and conflict is to establish clear priorities, rather than attempting to excel at everything. If you are certain where your priorities lie, you can decide which goals to concentrate on, and which activities can be relinquished or at least given less attention.

Exercise 5

Aim: Establishing priorities and goals

Below are a list of life goals. Assign a value to each one according to their priority in your life. Place a 1 in the column next to that area of your life which you value most, a 2 next to that which you value second and so on. This will help clarify where your priorities lie. Given that it is not practical to try to achieve everything at the same time, you can use this list to help you decide where to direct your energies. You may decide that the lowest priorities indicate that there are certain activities which you may have to reduce, or even eliminate, to enable you to achieve your major life goals.

Life values	*Priority*
Work	
Children	
Marriage	
Other family relationships	
Service to others	
Friendships	
Financial security	
Achievement	
Success	
Creativity	
Good health	
Independence	
Leisure activities	
Other (please specify)	

Having clarified your priorities it may be useful to consider some strategies for reducing overload from work or family or both.

Strategies for reducing overload

Questioning the need for long hours at work
If the family or other values are equal to or more important than your career, you may wish to question the need to put in long hours at work, to work overtime, or to bring work home in the evenings. A workaholic way of life is encouraged or expected in many organisations. It is difficult to challenge a corporate work ethic. Nevertheless, clear priorities may lead to decisions to reduce hours of work, at least for a short time, perhaps while children are young or an elderly relative is sick.

Delegation
There are usually two obstacles to the use of this strategy: a belief that we must do everything ourselves because nobody else can do it as efficiently, and a reluctance to relinquish power and control. Even if we do believe, perhaps justifiably, that nobody can perform our work as efficiently as we can, it is important to consider whether such a level of expertise is always necessary. If responsibilities are never delegated, other people will not develop the requisite skills.

The second obstacle, reluctance to relinquish power and control, suggests a feeling of insecurity and excessive competitiveness typical of the Type A stress prone personality (see Chapter

2). This type of attitude can itself contribute towards stress and should be avoided. The importance of delegation applies to family work as well as occupational demands, and is often rejected for the same two reasons: many women are reluctant to relinquish their ultimate control over home and children, and men are loath to give up the much greater power that goes with being the major breadwinner. As with work, it is only by tolerating other people's initial ineptness that part of one's domestic responsibility can eventually be delegated.

Lowering standards in the home: challenging the superwoman myth
Overload can be reduced by altering the demands in non-work areas of life. Given the problems associated with childcare discussed in earlier chapters, a decision may be made to have one child, or to have no children. If this is considered too high a price, a favoured strategy involves lowering of standards of domestic work. This means accepting that two partners with intense career involvement cannot compete with a full-time homemaker. It may involve questioning standards imposed by a couple's own parents. Often full-time homemakers are perfectionists, but it is necessary to ask if it is realistic to adopt such standards in addition to a full-time career. Below we consider some strategies for tackling the superwoman myth, based on the work of Abby King, Richard Winnett and Steve Lovett in the USA.[8]

- Do things effectively. This does not mean that they have to be done perfectly.
- Explore unrealistic beliefs. These may be that 'I have to be perfect at everything I do' or 'I have to spend every minute when I am not working, with my children', and they create stress.
- Set up priorities in domestic work and decide what compromises can be made.
- Ask yourself what will happen if you do not do everything perfectly. Are your fears realistic?
- Examine your guilt about childcare. Consider our discussion about the effects of working parents on children (Chapter 4). Is your guilt really justified?

Considering alternative ways of working
If family is a much greater priority than career or ambition, it may be useful to consider alternative ways of working (see Chapter 7). These could include not only those in place in your organisation, but also other possibilities which you may actively campaign for,

or encourage policy makers to consider. However, most strategies have both advantages and disadvantages, and these should be considered in the light of individual needs and circumstances.

Job sharing, in particular, may be worth considering, as many of the problems of part-time work are eliminated, because fringe

Table 8.1 *Alternative work patterns: advantages and disadvantages for employees*

Strategy	Advantages	Disadvantages
Part-time work	Enables parents to spend more time with children. Enables new parents to keep in touch with their career while children are young. Reduces overload and conflict. Creates flexibility.	Reduces income and other benefits. May reduce opportunities for promotion. Not usually available in high-level jobs. Often undertaken by women in addition to domestic responsibility – so less equality in marriage.
Working from home	Creates flexibility. Cuts down on travelling time. Facilitates return from maternity leave for women. May reduce childcare problems or schedule incompatibility. May be used to solve relocation problems.	May be limited opportunities. Partner at home may take greater share of domestic responsibility. May be reduced opportunities for promotion. Lack of social interaction with colleagues.
Job-sharing	Facilitates return from maternity leave for women. Reduces conflict between work and family. Reduces childcare problems. Creates flexibility. Could be available in a wide range of occupations at all levels. Fringe benefits are retained. (If both spouses job share) Increases equality and interdependence in marriage.	Reduced income (but not other benefits). Half a job tends to have more than half a workload. Difficulty in persuading some employers/ colleagues to implement.

benefits as well as salary are divided between the sharers. This option can be used to create opportunities in jobs and at levels which are not usually available on a part-time basis.

Case study

Let us examine the case of husband and wife job-sharing social workers: Lynda and John. When Lynda and John married, they were working as generic social workers. They were involved in union activity and in the drawing up of a project for job-sharing by the city council. This coincided with their wish to start a family. They began to job-share shortly before their first child was born. They now have two children. John covered for Lynda and worked full-time during her two periods of maternity leave. After each leave, Lynda returned to share the job and they shared the childcare between them. Recently, they successfully applied together for a new job as team leader. They each work for two or three days, on alternate weeks. Full consultation is provided for all team members at all times, but they split the staff for regular support and management. In order to ensure continuity they try to liaise with each other as much as possible, often reading each other's files and discussing work a great deal at home. They also make sure that they both attend team meetings, regardless of which half of the week they occur in. On the whole, they believe that the team feel that they benefit from having two managers.

They both consider that job-sharing has proved to be an ideal solution to the problems of combining career and family. According to John:

> It has enabled me to play a full part in bringing up the children. It is unusual for a man to have this opportunity and Lynda has had continuity in her career. We felt that it was important to look after the children ourselves while they were very young. We were able to do that. Overall it has worked well. Perhaps we do end up working more than half a week each to ensure a smooth transition, but it's a sacrifice that is well worth while.

Now that their children are a little older, they are able to use job-sharing for another purpose. Lynda is taking a further degree and John has once again taken over the job full-time to cover for her absence.

Assertiveness and work/family management

We have seen that the most effective strategies for managing work/family conflict and overload involve an attempt to change other people's expectations. The strategies require effective communication and negotiation which are a part of assertiveness skills. *Assertiveness* is the art of confident, clear, honest and direct communication, while at all times retaining respect for other people, and is an essential skill for those managing work and family demands. It is useful in transactions with family members, employers, colleagues and others. The assertive person is open and flexible and genuinely concerned about the rights of others, yet at the same time is able to establish his or her own rights. These include:

- The right to make mistakes
- The right to set one's own priorities
- The right for one's own needs to be considered as important as the needs of other people
- The right to refuse requests without feeling guilty
- The right to express oneself as long as this does not violate the rights of others
- The right to judge one's own behaviour, thoughts and emotions and to take the responsibility for the consequences.

Assertive behaviour is non-defensive and non-manipulative. The assertive person can be distinguished from aggressive individuals, who deny the rights of others, and from passive individuals, who deny their own rights. Examples of passive, aggressive and assertive responses to given situations are shown in Table 8.2

Assertive skills

Essential skills for assertive interaction include:

- Being able to decide what it is you want or feel and to say so specifically and directly.
- Sticking to your statement, repeating it, if necessary, over and over again.
- Deflecting any manipulative response from the other person which might undermine your assertive stance.
- Active listening.
- The ability to reach a joint solution.

Being specific
This means deciding what the point you want to make is and stating it without the unnecessary padding which we often use

Table 8.2 *Examples of passive, aggressive and assertive responses*

Situation	Passive responses	Aggressive responses	Assertive responses
Asking spouse to do more housework while you are busy on a work project.	I don't know how I'm going to manage all the housework while I'm so busy. (This is indirect – not asking openly for help.)	You know I've got a lot on at the moment, and you never pull your weight in the house. (Blaming other person – not taking responsibility.)	I am very busy at the moment. Can we sit down and discuss how we could rearrange the housework? (Provides opportunity for own needs discussion and gives reason.)
Asking to begin work half an hour later, because of nursery school hours.	It's really difficult for me to get to work for 9 but I'll try and make arrangements (Hoping for a concession – but not asking directly.)	There's no reason why I shouldn't be late for work sometimes. I do have family responsibilities, you know.	I am unable to be here before 9.30 because I have to drop my child at nursery at 9. Can we discuss how I can fit my work in? (Does not allow possibility of outright refusal by being reasonable, asking for a discussion.)
Refusing to do overtime/take on extra work.	I'd really rather not but I suppose if you can't get anybody else … (Does not accept own right to say 'no'.)	There must be other people you could ask. Why pick on me? (Does not accept other person's right to ask.)	No. I realise that you have a problem finding someone to do it, but I cannot do it at the moment. (Accepts other person's right to ask.)
A woman being asked at interview if she intends to have children.	I don't know. Maybe in a few years' time. (Accepts the question.)	You've no right to ask me that question. (Defensive – albeit technically correct.)	I'm sorry, I don't see the point of the question. You wouldn't ask a man. What is it that you are really asking? (Asks for clarification – tries to turn the question into a more direct assertive question, such as how long will you be working for us?)

when we are anxious or uncomfortable. Consider the statement below. The main point is underlined, the rest is padding.

> I know it's not good for people to take time off during the day, and I've never done it before but *I have to take my child to the doctors this afternoon*. He's got this awful rash and I'm quite worried about it.

Compare the impact of the specific statement, and the padded version. Padding tends to weaken the impact of a statement and confuse the listener.

Sticking to your statement, repeating if necessary
This involves a technique known as 'broken record'. Basically it is the skill of calm repetition. By repeating what you want to say over and over again, it is possible to ignore manipulative side-tracking and irrelevancies. Here is an example.

Parent	I don't feel that you are doing enough to help in the house. I would like you to put the washing in the machine in the mornings.
Teenage son	I haven't got time to do that.
Parent	I appreciate that you are rushed in the morning but I would like you to put the washing in.
Son	Other kids don't have to do that sort of thing.
Parent	I know different families have different routines but I would like you to put the washing on in the mornings.
Son	Well, it's not fair.
Parent	I'm sorry you don't think it's fair, but I would like you to put the washing on in the morning.

Fielding responses
This is the ability to indicate you have heard what the other person has said without being sidetracked from your main purposes. It is illustrated by the responses of the parent in the above dialogue and also in the following example.

1st colleague	Can you cover for me tonight?
2nd colleague	No, I'm sorry, I can't work late tonight.
1st colleague	But I've often covered for you in the past. I thought I could rely on you. (Attempt to manipulate by instilling guilt.)
2nd colleague	Yes, I appreciate that you have covered for me in the past (fielding), but I can't work late tonight.

Active listening

Assertive encounters are facilitated by active listening, that is, demonstrating that you have heard what the other person is saying. Sometimes this involves picking up emotions that may have been expressed through words or body language. For example, if you are being accused of not pulling your weight either at home or at work, rather than becoming defensive, which would exacerbate conflict, you can respond by saying, 'You seem very angry/disappointed'. This will help the other person to clarify what s/he feels and wants and you can then go on to discuss this constructively.

Negotiating a joint solution

If you present your point of view clearly and specifically, saying what exactly you want to happen, but also listen actively to what the other person is saying, it may become clear that there is a genuine gap between what you each want and need. You can then begin to work towards a joint solution, which is acceptable to both, that is, a win/win situation rather than a win/lose situation. In a win/lose situation, one person feels aggrieved and future conflict is guaranteed.

Using assertive skills to deal with work/family dilemmas

Assertive skills together with other work/family management skills can be applied in dealing with specific dilemmas, such as mobility, sexism and relationship problems.

Mobility – exploring possibilities and alternatives

It is often necessary for married couples, faced with the prospect of the relocation of one spouse, to deviate from accepted norms of behaviour. The traditional pattern is for the wife to move with her husband's job, while the husband moving with his wife's job is non-traditional. As we discussed in Chapter 3 , there are various strategies between these two extremes. Making your position clear from the outset may be one way of anticipating and avoiding future dilemmas. There is a range of positions which can be stated clearly upon taking up employment:

- Make it clear that you will not be willing to relocate
- Make it clear that you will not be willing to relocate unless a suitable position is also found for your spouse
- Make it clear from the outset that you are willing to relocate and that your family poses no obstacle. This may be particularly necessary for married women who may be passed

over for promotion on the assumption that they cannot be mobile.

- State that requests for relocation will be considered in the light of circumstances at the time, including your spouse's career situation, children's schooling and so on.

At a later stage, dilemmas may still arise. If so, there are a number of options, for example:

- Refuse to relocate. This may involve loss of promotion and will reflect your life priorities.
- If the new location is not too geographically distant, consider moving so that both of you can travel to work from one home which is approximately equidistant from your work locations. This may involve substantial travelling time.
- Consider alternating relocation decisions in each partner's favour. A move may be made now to facilitate one person's career on the understanding that the next move will favour the other spouse.
- Consider living apart during the week or for longer periods.
- Ask whether it is possible for one partner to work from home.
- Consider other creative solutions. Mary Maples[9] suggests that one solution may be for one partner to take up flying as a hobby!

Any decision will involve some sacrifice, in terms of career prospects, family life or travelling time. Your final decision will depend upon where your priorities lie in terms of your life values.

Forging new marital relationships
With shortage of time and energy and uneasiness about changing gender expectations among dual-earner spouses, resentment, anger and confusion can accumulate. Partners need to learn to communicate with each other and to be aware of each other's feelings. Unless there is a clear, open contract delineating the roles and responsibilities of each spouse, misunderstandings and conflicts may occur. Cary Cooper, Rachel Cooper and Lynn Eaker[10] suggest a strategy of semi-formalised family negotiation meetings in which all family members can be involved. This avoids conflicts and resentments by providing a clear action plan. They suggest a six stage role renegotiation strategy:

Step 1   Prepare a balance sheet of work and home commitments, listing details of hours spent and tasks undertaken.

Step 2 Call a formal family meeting to share concerns and discuss the detailed balance sheet.

Step 3 Renegotiate various family commitments.

Step 4 Create mutual action plans for the next three months which are agreed by all family members.

Step 5 Review success or otherwise of action plans at the end of a three-month period.

Step 6 Develop new action plans based on experience of previous one. Continue the process until all parties are satisfied with the arrangements.

If tensions within a family have already reached a stage of conflict and hostility, lack of effective communication between partners may preclude the possibility of renegotiating roles. It is necessary to find a way of reducing hostilities and reopening channels of communication. Here are some steps that can be taken:

● Find time to talk in a relaxed way. This may involve deliberately setting aside some time from busy schedules when lack of interruptions is guaranteed.

● Use assertive techniques for effective communication. Using the wrong words can alienate. It is better to take responsibility for your own feelings and behaviour than to accuse – for example, to say, 'I feel you could do more in the house' rather than 'You never do enough in the house'. Your feelings can be discussed, but an accusation merely makes the other person defensive.

● Listen to what the other person says. It is useful to reflect back, to show that you have really heard and accept his or her feelings. For example, 'It sounds as though you feel really angry with me. Can you tell me what it is that I do which makes you feel that way?'.

If problems have become really overwhelming:

● It might help to agree an official time out or call a temporary truce. A temporary separation, such as separate holidays, may provide time to work out a solution.

● Don't try to solve all problems at once. Work on one at a time.

● If necessary, elicit the help of a professional counsellor.

Countering sexism and discrimination at work
Knowing your rights is important in dealing with sexism and discrimination at work. If necessary, the help of the Equal

Opportunities Commission can be enlisted. However, the remedies are often financial settlements rather than restoration of career opportunities. It would be worthwhile considering how it might affect you as an individual before taking a stand. Women need to be prepared for the possibility of sexism and to anticipate how this can be dealt with. For instance, if personal questions about marriage and family are asked at interviews, how should this be dealt with? Below are some suggestions.

1. Point out that the question is discriminatory and refuse to answer. This is correct, but might be interpreted as aggressive.
2. Point out that the question is discriminatory, but be prepared to answer even so, in such a way as to assure the panel that there are no obstacles to you fulfilling all the duties required in the job.
3. Ask why the question is considered relevant. This is the most assertive reply and should force the interviewer to ask a more direct question, such as how long will you be working in this job? You can then point out that this depends on your success in the organisation.
4. Use the question to lead round to talking about your strengths. For instance, you might say that you have always employed a nanny because you worked such long hours in your previous job, or your husband has had to accept that your devotion to work leaves no time for children, or other people have commented that managing a career and family will pose no problems for someone with your organising skills.

The important point is not to be caught off-guard, but to be prepared for these questions, even though they should not arise.

Stress management training

While it may be possible to change our own ideas about the roles of men and women at home and at work, other people's attitudes may take a little longer to alter. Organisational expectations may also be resistant to change. In addition, there is always the possibility of short-term stress when the demands of work or family or both are particularly intense. It is useful to have ways of managing temporary or short-term stress. The exercises below can be used for group or individual stress management training.

Time management

When we asked dual-career spouses how they coped with their busy lifestyle their first reaction was usually to extol the virtues of good organisation. Attempting to do too much in a short space of time can create pressure. The best technique for reducing this stress may be to cut down on some of the tasks to be performed, but this is not always possible or desirable. The alternative is to use time management techniques which involve the balancing of supply and demand. By working out how to balance your demands with the time you have available, it is possible to schedule tasks into the most effective order and to avoid pressure.

Exercise 6

Aim: To draw up a balance sheet of time demands and supply.

Look at time demands:

1. List all tasks, both work and family, which need to be completed within a given time interval, such as for the following week.
2. Estimate how much time each task will take.
3. Increase the time estimates by 10–15 per cent to provide a margin of error for dealing with unexpected problems. If you set yourself too little time for each task, this will increase the pressure on you.

Then look at time supply:

1. For the week you are planning, identify the blocks of time available each day for completing necessary tasks. Deduct realistic times for travelling, eating, relaxing and so on.
2. Match the tasks to be accomplished with the time blocks available, so as to use the available time most constructively.
3. If you find there is not enough time available, work out priorities. List tasks in order of importance. Make sure that the most important task will be completed and leave the least important to be tackled only if extra time becomes available. An imbalance of supply and demand makes it apparent that some of the other active

---

strategies discussed earlier, such as delegation, must be considered. In determining the priority of tasks to be fitted into your busy time schedule, be aware of the importance of activities which reduce stress. Designating relaxation as a low priority may work on a very short-term basis, but will have adverse effects on your health in the long term as low priority tasks are rarely accomplished.

Recognising and modifying stress producing behaviour
The impact of certain personality characteristics and behavioural styles which can increase stress has been mentioned in earlier chapters. Foremost amongst these is the Type A behaviour pattern. It is well established that Type A individuals create stress for themselves at work, by imposing constant deadlines, refusing to delegate and by their competitiveness and aggressive personal style.[11] Type A behaviour is particularly incompatible with the dual-career lifestyle, as it usually leads to heavy workloads and a tendency to become so involved in work that other aspects of life are relatively neglected.[12] This type of behaviour increases the potential for interference between work and family. It may also spill over into the marital relationship, causing dissatisfaction and conflict.[13] In our study, Type A behaviour was one of the major causes of stress for dual-earners.

Training in the modification of Type A behaviour first encourages delegates to recognise the pattern in themselves and others, and then introduces ways of changing these responses. Several of the coping strategies discussed earlier, such as delegation, time management and developing assertiveness skills to enable people to say 'no' to additional work, are useful. In addition, there are a number of exercises based on behaviour modification techniques which can be used. These include encouraging Type A individuals to:

1. Set realistic goals about which aspects of their personality they can change and how long it might take.
2. Make a contract with themselves for each goal. Write it down and work on one modification at a time. Make these goals specific, for instance, 'For two weeks I will not stamp my feet and fume when queuing'.
3. Plan no more than they have time for.

4. Plan one event a week that puts friendship before work or encourages a sense of fun.
5. Rehearse situations which create anger or anxiety, and practise responding calmly.
6. Enlist help from family and friends in trying to change.
7. Find someone who is not Type A to serve as a role model.
8. Learn relaxation techniques to use under stress.
9. Look for subtle changes which show they are succeeding and reward themselves.

Cognitive reappraisal – perceiving the situation as non-stressful
An individual becomes stressed only if she or he appraises an event as stressful. It is stressful to feel helpless in the face of a potential threat, but the threat is reduced if an individual believes he or she can cope with the situation. This is why 'hardy' people remain healthy in the face of pressure.[14] They perceive their situation as meaningful, challenging and controllable.

There are several techniques which can be used cognitively to reappraise stressful situations. One technique involves comparing your own situation with alternatives, which might help to emphasise the advantages as well as the pressures in your chosen lifestyle. Margaret Paloma reported that the women in her study reduced tension by defining the dual-career pattern as favourable and advantageous in comparison with being a housewife.[15] Women who have spent time at home looking after small children often use this technique. Men who recognise the advantages of a dual-career marriage also compare themselves favourably with single breadwinners. However, other men compare themselves less favourably with the husbands of housewives, because of the extra domestic work which is expected of them. These men are more likely to become depressed, because they define their situation in a negative way.[16] Comparing yourself unfavourably with other people creates stress. It is important to select a realistic reference group to illustrate your own advantages, to instil a sense of control and challenge and to avoid feelings of disadvantage and self-pity.

Constructive self-talk is one technique which may be used to alter the appraisal of stressful events.[17] This refers to the words we say to ourselves, when confronted with challenging situations, which range from constructive and encouraging, to negative, harsh condemnation. Negative self-talk uses self-defeating words such as 'can't' and 'never'. This uses up emotional energy and achieves nothing, thereby promoting stress. Positive self-talk encourages a positive perception of situations and reduces stress. Table 8.3 lists examples of positive and negative self-talk.

Table 8.3   *Examples of positive/negative self-talk*

Situation	Negative self-talk	Constructive self-talk
Overload	I'll never get all this done.	There's a lot to do. I'll take one step at a time and it will be really satisfying when it is all finished.
After maternity leave	I'm so out of touch, I can't get back into the swing of things.	Everyone has some difficulty getting back to work. It'll take some effort, but I'll enjoy the challenge.
Marital conflict	Our marriage will never recover from this setback. He/she is impossible to live with.	We've been through a difficult patch but we can try and work it out.
Interview	I'm so nervous I can't think straight.	I'll take a deep breath and relax. Then I'll enjoy presenting myself in the best light.
Feelings of guilt	I shouldn't be working full time. I feel so guilty about leaving the baby. I'll always feel guilty.	There is no reason for me to feel guilty. The baby is in good hands at the nursery. Other children come to no harm and neither will mine.

Exercise 7

Aim: To practise the skill of constructive self-talk.

Write down the things you say to yourself in stressful situations. If you are using self-defeating negative self-talk, try to work out more constructive alternatives. These should be encouraging, but also realistic. You will not be convinced by something totally unrealistic, such as 'I'm going to give the most perfect performance imaginable', whereas a more modest 'I'll take a deep breath and do my very best' is encouraging and realistic.

Questioning irrational beliefs

Being realistic and rational in your beliefs is important in determining how you appraise situations. Irrational beliefs create stress. These include such beliefs as:

'I must be perfect at everything I do, otherwise I'm a failure.'

'Everybody must admire me.'

'I should be available to my child every minute of the day.'

'If our marriage is to be a success we should never, ever argue.'

Exercise 8

Aim: To question stress-producing irrational beliefs.

We have already discussed irrational beliefs which underlie the idea of the superwoman. Setting standards of personal behaviour which are impossible to achieve guarantees stress. Examine the 'musts' and 'shoulds' which govern your life, and ask yourself whether they are realistic and rational. If not, try to substitute more realistic expectations of yourself.

People sometimes become obsessed with negative self-talk, irrational beliefs, guilt or even rational anxiety. A solution to this involves the techniques of thought-stopping and mental diversion. *Thought stopping* involves visualising, or even saying out loud, the word 'Stop', as soon as you become aware of self-defeating thoughts. It should then be possible to switch to a pleasant, relaxing image, as a diversion from the disturbing thought. Dwell on this for 30–40 seconds, then slowly allow the demands of the real world back into your mind. If the anxiety returns, stop it in the same manner, and continue until the cycle of anxiety or guilt is broken.

Relaxation and meditation

One of the major complaints of dual-career spouses is extreme tiredness. For this reason, training in relaxation techniques is useful.

Transcendental meditation (TM) is a useful technique to help rid the body of tension. Meditation involves concentrating on a mantra, or single word, for approximately 20 minutes twice a day. This restricts one's mental and physical state and creates a tranquil state of mind and body. There is evidence that TM can eliminate stress, improve physical and mental health and increase efficiency.[18] Forty minutes a day may seem excessive to those with busy schedules, especially parents of young children. Nevertheless, the benefits of meditation should be considered when working out priorities and time management programmes. A more tranquil parent who is unavailable for 20 minutes twice a day may have more to offer his or her children than one who is constantly harassed. Meditation may also enable you to accomplish more in a shorter time because of improved performance.

Other useful relaxation techniques are progressive muscle relaxation and visualisation. Many commercially available tapes can be used to aid relaxation. Alternatively, you may relax by using the following simple procedure. Tense and then relax the muscles of each part of the body in turn: the left leg, right leg, left arm, right arm, lower half of the body, chest, shoulders, neck and face. Then, when the body is completely relaxed, visualise a pleasant scene, real or imaginary. Take your time doing this exercise and it will help to reduce tension and renew energy.

CONCLUSION

The effectiveness of developing work and family management skills will be constrained by the extent to which organisations themselves are changing. The aim of training programmes should be to facilitate change both at individual and organisational levels, rather than enabling individuals to cope with work and family demands in traditional systems. A primary objective of training is, therefore, to raise awareness of dual-career issues throughout the organisation, complementing rather than substituting for policy changes which recognise employees' family demands and responsibilities. Some of these changes are discussed in the next chapter.

REFERENCES

1. Quick, J C, Nelson, D J and Quick, J D (1990) *Stress and Challenge at the Top, The Paradox of the Healthy Executive*, Wiley, New York.
2. Rapoport, R and Rapoport, R N (1971) *Dual Career Families*, Penguin, London.

3. Hall, D T (1972) 'A model of coping with role conflict: The role behaviours of college educated women', *Administrative Science Quarterly*, 1, 7, 471–486.
4. Gilbert, L A, Holohan, C K and Manning, L (1981) 'Coping with conflict between professional and maternal roles', *Family Relations*, 319–426.
5. Alpert, D and Culbertson, A (1987) 'Daily hassles and coping strategies of dual earner and non dual earner women', *Psychology of Women Quarterly*, 11, 359–366.
6. Harrison, A O and Minor, J H (1978) 'Interrole conflict, coping strategies and satisfaction among black working wives', *Journal of Marriage and the Family*, 40, 799–805.
7. Yogev, S (1982) 'Are professional women overworked? Objective versus subjective perceptions of role loads', *Journal of Occupational Psychology*, 55, 3, 165–170.
8. King, A, Winnett, R and Lovett, S (1986) 'Enhancing coping behaviours in at risk populations', *Psychological Therapy*, 17, 57–66.
9. Maples, M (1981) 'Dual career marriages. Elements for potential success', *The Personnel and Guidance Journal*, September, 19–23.
10. Cooper, C L, Cooper, R D and Eaker, L (1988) *Living With Stress*, London: Penguin.
11. Price, V A (1982) *The Type A Behaviour Pattern. A Model For Research And Practice*, New York, Academic Press.
12. Price, V A (1982) ibid.
13. Burke, R J, Weir, T and Dulvors, R E (1979) 'Type A behaviour of administrators and wives' reports of marital satisfaction', *Journal of Applied Psychology*, 59, 9–14.
14. Kobasa, S C, Maddi, S R and Kahn, S (1982) 'Hardiness and Health: a Prospective study', *Journal of Health and Social Behaviour*, 42, 1, 168–177.
15. Paloma, M M (1972) 'Role conflict and the married professional woman', in C Safilios-Rothschild (ed), *Towards a Sociology of Women*, Lexington: Xerox College Publishing.
16. Schafer, R B and Keith, P M (1980) 'Equity and depression among married couples', *Social Psychology Quarterly*, 43, 4, 430–435.
17. Quick, J C and Quick, J D (1984) *Organizational Stress and Preventive Management*, New York: McGraw Hill.
18. Bloomfield, H H, Cain, G S, Jaffe, D T and Kory, R B (1976) *TM. How Meditation Can Reduce Stress*, London: Allen and Unwin.

9
Changing Organisations

Too many companies and businesses demand outrageous time commitments from those who work for them, without thought of the damage to family structure or for the strength their employees should get from a sound family life if they are allowed to foster it. (Alistair Burt MP, Junior Minister for Social Security, June 1993)

Perhaps one of the major benefits of the emergence and growth of the dual-career family may be the demand for a more balanced lifestyle. Both men and women want room in their lives for work and family. Large numbers of professionals and executives are no longer happy to devote their entire lives to the company, although many still do so reluctantly, and at considerable personal cost. As one male sales manager we interviewed suggested:

I don't think my firm recognise that I have family commitments – I am not sure that they even recognise that I'm human! I'm a robot to them, a machine which owes its loyalty and its time to the company.

Major changes have occurred within the family. Husbands and wives have careers and ambitions, but neither enjoys the support of a full-time helpmate. If both partners conform to the workaholic lifestyle demanded by many companies, there will be many dissatisfied families, as well as a highly stressed and, ultimately, inefficient, workforce. In the previous chapter we explored strategies which individuals can use to reduce and cope with the stress of the dual-career lifestyle, and the training implications. These techniques are unlikely to be effective if the workplace is unresponsive to the family needs of employees. Clearly, organisations have an important role to play in responding to the needs and expectations of today's workforce. Policies which were suitable for families in which there was a rigid division of labour are no longer appropriate.

Many large and successful companies are already acknowledging the need for change, and are leading the way by relinquishing traditional practices in favour of policies which accommodate the needs of families. In this chapter, we consider some of the organisational initiatives which may reduce the stress of the dual-career lifestyle. The once common experience of the sales manager quoted above ought soon to become a thing of the past.

CHALLENGING THE MALE MODEL OF WORK

Challenging the deep-seated tradition of companies which are organised around male workers with homemaker wives requires changes in attitudes as well as policies and practice. Many organisations provide childcare or part-time work, but continue to value and promote only those who work in a way which precludes any family involvement. The mission statement is a good place to start implementing company-wide change. Johnson and Johnson, one of many companies in the USA with broad work/family initiatives, has added to its company credo, 'We must be mindful of ways to help our employees fulfil their family obligations'. Research underpinning Business in the Community's campaign, *Opportunity 2000*, has identified four key aspects of good practice which have contributed to the successful implementation of equal opportunities, and to wider cultural change, within organisations in the UK, USA and Europe.[1] These are:

- **Commitment from the top**   Change must be led and championed by management, as part of overall strategic objectives.
- **Changing behaviour**   Change requires training, and must examine and tackle fundamental structure and behaviour of the organisation.
- **Building ownership**   Change is the responsibility of everyone in an organisation. Constant and effective communication is required to get the message across.
- **Making the investment**   Successful implementation of change requires the allocation of adequate resources, in terms of time, people and finance.

The alternative work patterns and provisions discussed in previous chapters, as well as initiatives discussed here, are most likely to assist members of dual-earner families in the context of changes in organisational culture which legitimise work/family boundaries at all levels.

LOCATION AND RELOCATION

In Chapter 3, we discussed some of the difficulties encountered by dual-career couples when they are seeking jobs and having to agree on a mutually acceptable location. Organisations can assist dual-career couples by changes in their recruitment and hiring policies. As the number of professionals in dual-career marriages continues to grow, organisations will increasingly need to attract dual-career couples in order to recruit the best candidates. A recent study of 827 managers in the USA[2] showed that a major factor determining employees' willingness to relocate was the willingness of their spouses to do likewise. However, spouses are not necessarily men, and employed. Women were as willing as men to relocate, but were given fewer oportunities. The implication is that if companies are to ensure a large pool of flexible managers, willing to move when necessary, they need to provide career development opportunities for women, as well as support systems for spouses. Uma Sekaran makes a number of recommendations to organisations working to adapt to the changes in the nature of the potential workforce.[3]

- Some companies operate anti-nepotism policies which prevent the hiring of dual-career couples if their relationship is known. Such policies are outmoded and should be discarded; they not only create the potential for location dilemmas for dual-career spouses, but may also deprive organisations of the talents of highly suitable recruits.
- Often organisations are loath to hire the spouse of an employee in a rival company, because of a presumed conflict of interests. A case brought to an Industrial Tribunal concerned a woman who complained of unfair dismissal after marrying an employee of a rival firm.[4] The Tribunal's findings that she had been discriminated against on the basis of marital status was not upheld by the Court of Appeal. Nevertheless, such practices can discriminate against married professionals. Sekaran suggests that organisations do away with conflict of interest policies by incorporating an oath of loyalty into employee contracts. In practice, she argues, couples seem to have evolved their own codes of professional conduct to protect both their own careers and the interests of the employing company.
- Advertising procedures can be altered to attract dual-career couples. Companies should advertise the broadest possible

range of job opportunities to increase the scope for partners to find positions simultaneously. In addition, advertisements could specify that dual-career couples are acceptable to an organisation and that policies which facilitate the combining of careers and family, such as childcare or flexible working arrangements, are available.

- A interviewing strategy should be adopted to assess ability and potential of candidates and avoid biased assumptions, particularly relating to married women. Questions about her husband's job, although unlawful, are frequently asked. Decisions should not be made on the assumption that the husband will be the major breadwinner.
- Mechanisms for training interviewers should be established. Interview panels should include members of dual-career families and high ranking people in the organisation to ensure objectivity and fairness.

Once a couple have been appointed to jobs within a specific location, there is no guarantee that their problems have ended. At middle and senior management levels, promotional decisions are often based on mobility. Even for single earners, the psychological and social costs of frequent moves are considerable.[5] Dual-career couples have the added difficulties of deciding whether to refuse a move because of the spouse's job, of finding a new job for a spouse, or adjusting to living apart as a commuter couple. Most companies recognise employees' needs for financial assistance with moving, but dual-career issues are only just beginning to be acknowledged. A study of corporate relocation policies in the USA undertaken by Catalyst in the mid-1980s reported that most of the business executives surveyed recognised that dual-career couples might have problems, but had no idea how many of their employees were in dual-career marriages.[6] Most admitted that dual-career issues were not addressed in their company practices. Nevertheless, companies are becoming more aware of relocation as a potential obstacle, particularly as more men, as well as women, refuse to relocate. Policies for dealing with this issue are at least being operated by some organisations. There are several possibilities:

- Organisations should, first, question whether their relocation policy is necessary. Is it essential for managers to gain experience in a wide range of locations, or could more promotions be made within one area?
- Employees who are single, or whose spouses are also ready

for a move, may welcome a change of location; but dual-career spouses should not be compelled to compete with those in different family circumstances. A more liberal attitude could be taken towards those who refuse to relocate, so that this does not prejudice their opportunities of promotion later in their careers.

- Organisations operating a policy of hiring both members of dual-career couples could, by careful planning, arrange the relocation of the couple as a unit.

- The most widely adopted policy among companies which recognise the problem is to offer assistance in finding a job for the spouse of the relocated employee. This may take the form of financial assistance for job-seeking or more direct help, such as arranging job interviews. Organisations can research and make inventories of the career opportunities for partners in a particular location, or form a consortium of companies to create a job bank. Eventually, computer-assisted job searches may ease the trauma of relocation decisions.

- Counselling and advisory services are also offered to some families. Counselling and workshops are often conducted to help executives and their families cope with the stress of relocation. However, these tend to focus on traditional single-earner families rather than dual-career couples.[7] Counselling services geared towards dual-career families may help employees to deal with difficult decisions, feelings of guilt and the emotional stress of relocation policies.

- Flexible and alternative work schedules can all be used to assist relocated employees or their spouses. If a decision has been made to live apart and commute, a compressed working week and three-day weekend reduce the time apart, while telecommuting will allow one partner to be flexible in terms of relocating with his or her spouse.

OPPORTUNITIES FOR WOMEN

Most organisational 'policies for women' focus on the provision of childcare, flexible working arrangements or career-break schemes to ease their domestic burden. In fact, these are policies for families, since both women and men have domestic obligations. It is true that initiatives such as these help women, because they often bear the major brunt of childcare. Domestic responsibilities, however, are not the only barriers to equal opportunities. As we discussed in Chapter 6, gender stereotypes can be particularly damaging, shaping management expectations and preventing women from achieving their full potential.[8] Most organisations, reflecting the wider society, are patriarchal and male-dominated. Judi Marshall, writing about the experiences of female managers, argues that although organisations appear to have changed on the surface by accepting more women into senior positions, the characteristics and modes of behaviour which they value are still based on the male norm.[9]

Women, therefore, remain at a substantial disadvantage. They are often expected to behave differently from men, yet they are judged by male standards. As many of the women we interviewed attested, they generally have to out-perform men in order to achieve recognition and success. It is often said that sexual equality will exist when a mediocre woman is promoted! Obstacles to women's career progress need to be removed to eliminate the waste of talent. Promoting equal opportunities at work will also help to increase women's bargaining power at home, as high-earning women are in a better position to demand equal domestic participation by their husbands.

How can organisations promote opportunities for women?

Eliminate stereotypes
Male and female employees are more alike than they are different. Beliefs that all women are unreliable, or cannot be tough, take risks, or display leadership ability, must be challenged. Some women, as well as some men, display these characteristics. However, stereotypes are apt to become self-fulfilling. A woman who is expected to be responsible and enterprising is much more likely to behave in this way than one who is expected to lack these qualities. Workshops or discussion groups can help to identify stereotypes and examine their impact on women's personal development and organisational advancement (see Chapter 6).

Avoid discrimination at selection and appraisal interviews
The Equal Opportunities Commission issues guidance notes for interviewers. Interviews should deal only with the applicant's suitability for the job. Questions about marriage plans or family intentions should not be asked. If information is necessary for personnel records, it can be collected after a job offer has been made.

Avoid sexist language
If managers are always referred to as 'he' in organisational

publications and communications, this will reinforce the view that management is a male domain. Similarly, it is demeaning to refer to adult women as 'girls', although this is not an uncommon practice.

Provide role models
Attempts should be made to promote a substantial number of women, rather than a token woman or two, to senior posts. This can be achieved through a positive action programme. Not to be confused with positive discrimination, this involves policies to enhance women's opportunities. Many British organisations are appointing equal opportunity officers and implementing successful policies. For example, the Littlewoods organisation has a policy which includes improving recruitment and promotion practices, equal opportunity training for men and women, removing the requirement for relocation except within a restricted locality, and specific promotion targets for minority groups. The result has been an increase in the number of women at all levels of management.

Examine promotional policies and eliminate double standards
Women often achieve promotion to middle management, but are then blocked by what has been termed a 'glass ceiling' beyond which they find it difficult to progress.[10] Frustrated by lack of advancement, many women leave large organisations at this stage, often to start their own entrepreneurial ventures.[11] Barriers are often the consequence of women having to reach higher standards than men in order to achieve recognition. Organisations should endeavour to identify and eliminate informal policies based on this double standard.

Provide training aimed specifically at women
Positive action campaigns often include training courses aimed specifically at women in assertiveness, personal effectiveness, career planning and other skills (see Chapter 7). However, this is not uncontroversial. Some women feel that these courses are primarily remedial and are detrimental to progress because women are singled out and made to appear to need extra help.[12] Nevertheless, other women find such courses helpful and they should be available for those who feel they could benefit from them. It is worth noting that girls achieve more in single-sex schools than in co-educational ones, where boys command the greater share of attention.[13] The same principle may well apply in corporate training.

Eliminate 'old boy networks'
Women often miss out by exclusion from old-boy networks in male-dominated organisations or professions. For instance, a recent publication by the Policy Studies Institute provides evidence that this is prevalent in the medical profession.[14] It ensures that vacant posts go to members of the network, who are predominantly white, male and Oxbridge-educated. Rigorous scrutiny of areas where women are under-represented should attempt to root out the effects of these influences.

Provide support groups for women
Women in a male-dominated environment often feel isolated. Women's networks and support groups can help to overcome this problem and provide a forum in which women can share experiences. One multinational company established a women's group with the full support of the senior personnel manager.[15] The group aimed to help women realise their career aspirations and assist management and the training department in providing career advice. Such a group enables issues of particular concern to women to be identified, so that action can be taken.

Recognise and value women's contributions to the organisation
Although it is important to eliminate stereotyped views about 'typical' women and men, organisations should avoid falling into the trap of expecting women to emulate men. Women's experiences as an undervalued group in society and within organisations inevitably shape a different identity. Judi Marshall argues that, until recently, women in management have had the choice of either conforming to female stereotypes by adopting caring or helpmate roles, or else imitating the behaviour of male managers.[16] Now, she argues, they are beginning to forge a middle road between the two extremes. Management training should encourage women to develop their own styles of behaviour, as well as help men to feel less threatened and more supportive of their female colleagues.

Monitor progress of equal opportunities programmes
Equal opportunities programmes must be carefully monitored to ensure that they are achieving their goals. Several organisations and professions claim to be equal opportunities employers, but have failed to remove bias and ambivalent attitudes to women.[17] Lack of promotion can be particularly damaging to the self-esteem of women in an institution which claims, unjustifiably, to be an equal opportunities employer, because people tend to

regard this claim as representing the truth.[18] Even companies such as Littlewoods, with established equal opportunities policies, recognise the need to keep this continually under review.

Counselling

As dual-career members attempt to achieve a balance between careers and family, a number of dilemmas arise. Although spouses may be able to offer each other mutual support, it is often necessary to have a neutral, third person to turn to in order to sound out feelings about parenthood, competition between partners, ambivalence about gender expectations, relocation and other important issues. A professional counsellor may also be needed to help some couples work out marital conflicts resulting from one or both partners' intense job involvement. Counsellors who are familiar with an organisation's policies, and also have an understanding of dual-career issues can be of great assistance in helping couples or individual spouses to examine their own values and priorities and also to enable them to reconcile areas of conflict.

Employee assistance and counselling programmes (EAPs) have been established in a number of American organisations. These take the forms of in-house organisational counselling, contracts with outside counselling agencies, or a 24-hour telephone line for personal counselling. Such initiatives are also beginning to spread to the UK, where several companies now provide some form of counselling service. In the mid-80s, the Post Office introduced organisational counsellors in two regions. The counsellors helped employees with a range of problems related to the workplace, as well as domestic situations and stress and health problems. A study[19] evaluating this service found that sickness absence events and days lost to sickness declined by 49 per cent and 66 per cent respectively from six months before to six months after counselling. In addition, there was a significant decline in employee anxiety, depression and psychosomatic symptoms after counselling, and a significant rise in self-esteem. Twenty-five per cent of the employees presented with marital or family problems, and a further 24 per cent with mental ill health effects stemming partly from marital and dual-career conflicts.

Organisational counsellors currently tend to assist employees in dealing with life crises, such as divorce and bereavement, coping with health problems and managing stress at work. If counselling programmes are to be extended to help dual-career couples, those involved need to be aware of the particular issues faced by these individuals. Concern has also been expressed that counsellors should not be biased against dual-career couples in general, or against dual-career wives or husbands in particular.[20]

In addition to counselling individuals and couples, assistance programmes can help by facilitating self-help groups and workshops. Counsellors are in a unique position to identify problems shared by a number of employees and to assist in establishing self-help and support groups. Finally, counsellors can establish programmes to prevent stress relating to transitions and stressful life events. Preparation for transitions such as new parenthood could help dual-career spouses to anticipate potential problems and to consider appropriate coping strategies. Some organisations already prepare employees for retirement. The pressures associated with the transition to parenthood for dual-career couples should be recognised and assistance offered at all stages.

WIDER SOCIETAL CHANGES AND ORGANISATIONAL POLICIES

In spite of gloomy predictions that women's careers would bring about the demise of the family, dual-earner families are now established as viable and potentially highly satisfying. Nevertheless, traditional norms and values, rooted in centuries of male dominance and female subordination, persist. Changes in attitudes concerning gender roles, professional life and organisational structures cannot be expected to occur all at once. They will evolve over time, as each generation is reared by parents who subscribe to more egalitarian family values. Until the necessary structures and supports develop in organisations and in the wider society, we remain in a period of transition and some transitional stress is inevitable. Throughout this book we have argued that society's view of women's and men's roles, together with organisational expectations and the reluctance of some men to translate beliefs about equality into support in the home, create tensions for dual-career members. As long as initiatives for change are left to individuals, progress will be piecemeal. Clearly, changes in organisational and social policy are also required.

In the late 1960s and early 1970s the political demands of the women's liberation movement included equal pay and opportunities at work, paid maternity leave and free childcare. How far have these goals been achieved? There is legislation on equal pay and discrimination, but equality at work and within the home remains an ideal rather than a reality, although some progress is being made. Paid maternity leave is still inadequate and the notion of parental leave so prevalent in continental Europe, which enables both parents to share early childcare, has yet to be accepted in the UK. There has been no progress on free childcare for all. The belief that childcare is a private matter, best undertaken by mothers in their own homes, remains widespread in the UK, and underpins the reluctance of policymakers to support such provision.

The European Commission, which has consistently shown commitment to equal opportunities in the labour market, recognises that the reconciliation of work and family is a necessary condition for this to happen. It also recognises that this requires social partnerships, especially between government and employers. Both, together with trades unions, can work to promote, not just equal opportunities at work, but also the sharing of family care by men and women. The British government, and employers, should give serious consideration to the following policy issues.

Better maternity leave rights and facilities

Maternity rights and facilities are essential to enable women to combine continuous careers with childrearing. Legislation in the 1970s provided women with protection against dismissal on the grounds of pregnancy, and with the right to reinstatement during the period ending 29 weeks after the birth. However, the qualifying conditions for maternity rights exclude many women, unlike in other EC countries where fewer restrictions apply. The government in the UK is concerned that small businesses should be protected from the 'burden' of maternity leave which, it is suggested, might make them reluctant to employ women of childbearing age.[21] Although some employers do display such reluctance, this is due more to prejudiced attitudes than to experience. A survey of the impact of maternity leave shows that most employers report no difficulties concerning maternity rights and, in fact, fewer small firms than large organisations report problems in this area.[22]

We have quoted examples of employers who break the law by failing to reinstate women. Stiffer penalties may deter such actions in the future. Women who are found to be the victims of unlawful dismissal should be entitled to automatic reinstatement.

Financial problems during maternity leave also create stress for some dual-career couples. The six weeks' earnings related benefit is the shortest in Europe. A flat-rate statutory maternity pay is less than full pay and is provided for only 18 weeks. Any further leave has to be taken without pay. This can cause difficulties, particularly for women who are the major breadwinners or for those whose income is essential for items such as mortgage repayments. Consequently, many women are obliged to return to work before they feel ready to do so, often working hours that are disruptive to family life. This is not in the best interests of parents, children or organisations. Most European countries ensure some financial support for the duration of maternity leave. Payment throughout maternity leave reduces the burden on dual-career families and provides women with a more realistic choice about how much leave to take. A number of forward-looking employers now recognise the limitations of current provision and offer additional benefits, such as the right to return to work after maternity leave after one (rather than two) years' full-time service, reduction in the qualifying period for part-time staff, up to 25 weeks' leave on full pay, and the right to work part-time after maternity leave.

'New daddy days'

Fathers in the UK have no statutory rights to take time off work for the birth of their child, although many employers provide paid leave. Given that most fathers attend the birth of their children nowadays, such provision is essential. A study of fathers' attitudes to paternity leave, published by the Equal Opportunities Commission, revealed that 91 per cent favoured the introduction of paid paternity leave.[23] In Sweden fathers are allowed ten days' leave at the time of the birth of their children, known as 'new daddy days', in addition to other parental leave entitlement. This is primarily intended to allow fathers to care for older siblings, but it is also extensively used by fathers without older children. Unlike parental leave described below, leave can be taken by both parents simultaneously at this important early stage of family bonding.

Parental leave

Essential though maternity leave and paternity leave at the time of the birth are, the present system perpetuates the notion that childcare is primarily the mother's responsibility. It also discriminates against the increasing number of fathers who want to participate fully in the care of their children. Parental leave should also be available to enable parenting to be shared during infancy. The notion of parental leave which does not discriminate between mothers and fathers was introduced in Sweden in 1973, to promote opportunities for married and cohabitating women and to ensure the welfare of children. Before 1973 Swedish mothers were entitled to six months' paid maternity leave. Under the parental leave system, fathers and mothers are entitled to a total of one year's leave in any form which best suits their needs. Only one parent at a time stays at home, and the leave may be taken on a part-time basis and extended accordingly. Parents receive benefits equivalent to 90 per cent of earnings. As the benefit is financed by the National Social Insurance Board employers are not directly affected financially.

The British government has resisted EC pressure to legislate on parental leave, arguing that this is inappropriate and that arrangements should be left to individual negotiations. At best, this leads to uneven and inadequate provision. Concern has also been expressed about the costs of implementing parental leave rights. However, most European countries have introduced some form of statutory parental leave. In general, this is seen as a means of creating new, short-term contracts for some of the population, while allowing women to minimise disruption to their careers. Part of the costs of introducing these rights into the UK could be offset by the creation of jobs and removal of several thousand people each year from the unemployment register. A House of Lords Select Committee found no convincing evidence that the proposal for parental leave would raise the costs of industry.[24] The Select Committee estimated that parental leave would affect less than 1 per cent of male employees in any one year and only 2 per cent of employed women, which is minimal compared with other reasons for absence. As Lady Platt, the then Chair of the Equal Opportunities Commission, declared during the House of Lords debate, 'If women and men can be helped to attend to their families and continue in employment for the benefit of the prosperity of the country, can we afford *not* to introduce this legislation?'

At first, it is unlikely that the majority of men would take advantage of their entitlement to parental leave, because of the lack of role models and because their absences might not be widely sanctioned by colleagues and supervisors. Even in Sweden, behaviour remains more traditional than official policy, with more women than men taking their full leave entitlement.

Nevertheless, there is evidence that changes in family roles are beginning to occur. Swedish men with high-earning wives are particularly likely to take parental leave, again illustrating the importance of equal opportunities at work in bringing about changes in domestic roles.

In the absence of legislation on parental leave, many organisations are responding by introducing a system of leave for parents, including those with adoptive children or by career-break schemes which, at least in principle, are available to either parent.

Leave for family reasons

The EC also recommends that employees should be able to claim a specific number of days' paid leave each year for pressing family reasons, such as the illness of a spouse, child, or person who usually cares for the child. Some organisations already make this provision, and legislation may ultimately be introduced to provide this right for all employees, again following the lead of most European countries. This would encourage fathers to share more equally a burden which has hitherto exerted a much greater impact on women's working lives. The lack of paid leave in the case of a child's illness is based on the view that mothers are, or should be, at home, or that their income is non-essential, and this is a source of considerable pressure for dual-career parents. The reality of women's careers, and the joint responsibility of men and women for parenting, needs to be fully acknowledged by government and organisations, recognising the links between work and family.

CHILDCARE AND SOCIAL POLICY

Our children are our future and, of course, we cannot afford to neglect them. However, it is a common misconception that employed mothers do just that. Certainly, children need time with both their parents. Parental leave and working days which are not too long would help families. However, infants do not need to be with their mother (or father) for 24 hours a day. Indeed, as we discussed in chapter 4, there is now evidence that children actually benefit from having working parents, provided that they have good quality day care. The current state of provision of pre-school childcare in the United Kingdom is among the worst in Europe, with demand far exceeding supply. If lives of dual-career and dual-earner families are to be improved, good quality, affordable childcare must be widely available. Assistance with childcare provided by companies is important, although ultimately statutory changes may be necessary.

One advantage of the state provision of childcare is that standards of nurseries can be monitored. The government could assist working parents by extending tax benefits beyond workplace nurseries to other forms of childcare assistance. The requirement for large organisations or business conurbations to provide a nursery before they receive planning permission would be another logical and welcome step forward.

Dual-career couples in Britain are currently faced with a dilemma about whether to remain childless or to risk the consequences of combining employment and parenting in a society which is still ambivalent about mothers pursuing serious careers. While some couples will always choose voluntary childlessness, others reluctantly sacrifice parenthood to their careers. Better childcare provision and parental leave entitlements would help to ease the path for the majority of couples who do not wish to forgo parenthood. However, given the increasing number of women pursuing professional and executive careers, the lack of such provision may well ensure that dual-career marriages are the 'ultimate contraceptive of the future'.[25]

Care of the elderly and the disabled

The changing age structure of the population is already causing concern among those responsible for services for the elderly.[26] Illness or infirmity among elderly parents or other relatives can create great problems for dual-career spouses. The care of the elderly or sick, like the care of children, is generally assumed to be the responsibility of female members of the family. Many women are forced into part-time employment to enable them to care for sick relatives. Others bear the burden of guilt if they sustain a full-time commitment to their careers. As with childcare, improved services for the elderly, by both employers and the government, is also important for dual-career spouses. Recent legislation on care in the community relies heavily on informal carers, most of whom will also be in employment.[27] Employees may find it increasingly difficult to manage their work and caring responsibilities – for the elderly, for adult children with disabilities, and other dependents – in this climate.

EQUAL OPPORTUNITIES AT WORK AND AT HOME

This book has highlighted the fact that women's domestic responsibilities can reduce their career opportunities. Women's secondary position in the workforce weakens their bargaining position in the home, creating a vicious circle of inequality. It is not possible to legislate for domestic relationships, but effective equal opportunity legislation should, ultimately, bring about changes in family roles. Women who achieve high occupational status and earnings are in a better position to expect equal domestic participation by their partners.

Legislation which prohibits direct and indirect discrimination against women has been an important step towards recognising and acting upon the principle of equality for women. Nevertheless, the position of women in the labour force has changed little. Women are still in the minority in all but the traditionally female (lower paid and lower status) professions, and although the number of women entering male-dominated occupations is growing they are still vastly under-represented in senior positions. Many employers continue to discriminate, knowingly or unknowingly, and women still feel they have to be better than men to be promoted. It is clear that there is a need for stronger commitments from organisations (along the lines of *Opportunity 2000*) or legislation to force equal opportunities. Existing legislation does not require employers to produce a policy for positive action. Employers should be required actively to promote equal opportunities and to demonstrate that they are complying with this demand. More forceful legislation towards 'affirmative action' exists in the USA, where organisations in receipt of government grants or contracts must follow a positive recruitment strategy in the employment of women and minority groups or else lose government support.

Equality of opportunity should also be extended to part-time workers. At present, the majority of these are women, but men and women should be able to choose to work shorter hours while they have young children, without loss of promotion rights. Protective legislation applying to full-time workers should be extended to all part-time employees and steps should be taken to ensure that part-timers are not excluded from benefits (on a pro rata basis) and from access to training and promotion. The principle of non-discrimination between full-time and part-time workers has been endorsed by the EC and some UK organisations are now taking these steps. The right to work shorter hours without loss of seniority or opportunity during the early parenting years is essential for dual-career families.

Despite the government's opposition to EC recommendations at present, its policies on maternity, paternity, parental and family leave, childcare and eldercare, and equal opportunities may be improved in due course. Meanwhile, employers who understand the needs of the new workforce and the implications for management of the workplace revolution, will lead the way.

REFERENCES

1. Hammond, V and Holton, V (1991) *A Balanced Workforce. Achieving Cultural Change For Women: A Comparative Study*, Ashridge Management Research Group.
2. Brett, J M, Stroh, L K and Reilly, A H (1993) 'Pulling up roots in the 1990s: who's willing to relocate? *Journal of Organizational Behaviour*, 14, 49–60.
3. Sekaran, U (1986) *Dual Career Families. Contemporary Organizational and Counselling Issues*, San Francisco: Jossey Bass.
4. See the case of Coleman v Skyrail Oceanic Ltd, Court of Appeal, 1981.
5. Cooper, C L (1982) *Executive Families Under Stress*, Englewood Cliffs: Prentice-Hall.
6. Catalyst (1983) *Corporate Relocation Practices: A Report on a Nationwide Survey*, New York.
7. Kamerman, S B and Kahn, A J (1987) *The Responsive Workplace. Employers and a Changing Labor Force*, New York: Columbia University Press.
8. Davidson, M and Cooper, C L (1992) *Shattering the Glass Ceiling: the Woman Manager*, London: Paul Chapman.
9. Marshall, J (1987) 'Issues of identity for woman managers', in Clutterbuck, D and Devine, M (eds) *Businesswomen*, Basingstoke: Macmillan.
10. Morrison, A, White, R and Van Velson, E (1987) *Breaking the Glass Ceiling*, California: Addison-Wesley.
11. Foster, J and Carson, L (1988) 'Balancing work and home', in *Women in Management. Optimising the Potential*, Berkhamsted, Herts: Ashridge Management College.
12. Handy, R (1988) In *Women in Management. Optimising the Potential*, op. cit.
13. Stanworth, M (1981) *Gender and Schooling. A study of Sexual Divisions in the Classroom*, London: Hutchinson.
14. Allen, I (1988) *No Room at the Top. A Study of Doctors and their*

Careers, London: Policy Studies Institute.
15. Truman, C (1986) *Overcoming the Career Break: A Positive Approach*, Manchester: UMIST.
16. Marshall, J (1987) op. cit.
17. Spencer, A and Podmore, D (1987) *In a Man's World. Essays on Women in Male Dominated Professions*, London: Tavistock.
18. McCauley, J (1987) 'Women academics: A case study in inequality', in Spencer, A and Podmore, D, op. cit.
19. Cooper, C L, Sadri, G, Allison, T and Reynolds, P (1990) 'Stress counselling the Post Office', *Counselling Psychology Quarterly*, 3 (1), 3–11.
20. Rice, D G (1987) *Dual-Career Marriage, Conflict, and Treatment*, New York: Macmillan.
21. *Building Businesses ... Not Barriers* (1986) Government White Paper.
22. Daniel, W W (1981) 'Employers' experiences of maternity rights legislation', *Department of Employment Gazette*, July.
23. Bell, L, McKee, L and Priestly, K (1983) *Fathers, Childbirth and Work*, Manchester: Equal Opportunities Commission.
24. House of Lords Select Committee on the European Communities Parental Leave and Leave for Family Reasons (1985) London: HMSO.
25. Hootsmans, M (1992) 'Beyond 1992: Dutch and British corporations and the challenge of dual-career couples' in Lewis, S, Izraeli, D N and Nootsmans, M (eds) op. cit.
26. Hunt, A (1988) 'The effects of caring for the elderly and infirm on women's employment', in Hunt, A (ed), *Women and Paid Work. Issues of Equality*, London: Macmillan.
27. Laczko, F and Noden, S (1993) 'Combining paid work with eldercare: the implications for social policy' in *Health and Social Care in the Community*, Oxford: Blackwell.

Appendix

Questionnaire

Example of a questionnaire used to survey organisational family needs.

Section A

1. Age   ☐ Under 25

                 ☐ 26–35

                 ☐ 35–45

                 ☐ Over 45

2. Job description   . . . .

    Office   . . . .

3. Do you have any children?   ☐ Yes

                                    ☐ No

4. Sex   F ☐   M ☐

If you do not have children but may wish to have a child at some later date, or if your family is not yet complete, please answer the questions in Section B. If your family is complete please answer Section C.

Section B

1. If you have a baby at some time in the future which of the following statements would best describe your career intentions? (Please tick one number.)

☐ I would definitely want to return to my job after maternity leave.

☐ I would like to return to part-time work after maternity leave.

☐ I would like to take a break and return to work after a few years.

☐ I would definitely not want to return to work in the foreseeable future.

☐ I am undecided.

There are a number of changes which could be introduced to make it easier to manage work and family. We would like to know how useful you think these initiatives might be, and how likely it is that you would take advantage of them.

2. *Career break schemes*
   These are schemes which would allow you to take a break of not more than five years for childrearing and to return to your job without any loss of seniority. You would be expected to undertake at least two weeks' paid work with the company each year and you would be provided with information packs during your absence. How likely is it that you would take advantage of this scheme if it were to be introduced?

   ☐ Extremely Unlikely ☐ Unlikely ☐ Undecided ☐ Likely

   ☐ Extremely Likely

   If you think a career break scheme would be useful would you prefer:

   ☐ One five-year break

   ☐ Two shorter breaks

3. *Childcare*
   Which of the following childcare options would be most useful to you?

   ☐ A nursery in or near the office.

   ☐ An allowance to contribute towards the cost of childcare.

   ☐ An information and referral service which would provide assistance in finding a nanny, nursery, etc.

4. If an on-site or nearby nursery were to be provided, how likely is it that you would use it in preference to other forms of childcare?

   ☐ Extremely Unlikely ☐ Unlikely ☐ Undecided ☐ Likely

   ☐ Extremely Likely

5. *Alternative Work Schedules*
   Please indicate how useful you think you would find each of the following alternatives if you have a young child. (1 = no use at all, 2 = not very useful, 3 = not sure, 4 = useful, 5 = extremely useful.)

   ☐ Flexitime (full-time hours at times to suit you)

   ☐ Working from home

☐ Part time work

☐ Opportunity to job share

6. Which would be your preferred option, if any?

     . . . .

7. Which would be the most helpful in enabling you to continue with your career after having children:

     ☐ A career break

     ☐ Childcare assistance

     ☐ Alternative work schedules

8. Do you have any other comments or suggestions?

Section C

To be completed if you already have children.

1. How many children do you have?   . . . .

2. What ages are they   . . . .

3. Did you take maternity/paternity leave when your children were born?

     ☐ Yes

     ☐ No

4. What age were your children when you returned to full-time work?

     . . . .

5. If you returned to part-time work, what age were your children when you began work?

     . . . .

6. Career break scheme (for description see Section B question 2)

     How likely is it that you would have taken advantage of such a scheme if it had been available?

     ☐ Extremely Unlikely   ☐ Unlikely   ☐ Undecided   ☐ Likely

     ☐ Extremely Likely

7. *Childcare*
   What form of childcare do you use/did you use when your children were young?

   . . . .

8. Which of the following options would you find most useful/ would you have found most useful when your children were young?

   ☐ A nursery in or near the office

   ☐ An allowance to contribute towards the cost of childcare

   ☐ An information and referral service which would provide assistance in finding a nanny, nursery etc.

9. If you have young children, would you make use of an on-site or nearby nursery?

   ☐ No   ☐ Unlikely   ☐ Not sure   ☐ Probably   ☐ Yes

10. What other policies would help you to balance your career with family?

Index

after-school programmes 84, 91–2
aggressiveness 144, 145
alternative working arrangements
    34, 120–4, 141–3 Table 8.1
androgyny 26
appraisal interviews 71
assertiveness 144–7
    training 29–30, 34, 115
    in work-family dilemmas
        147–50
    and work-family management
        143–4

'breadwinner ethic' see male work
    ethic
business trips 13
    and sexuality 113

camps for children 84
care in the community 87, 172
career break schemes 127–9
career counselling 54
career development, issues in
    36–56
career paths, alternative, for
    women 71
career planning
    flexibility 37–8
    for women 71
career/life planning courses 134
careers
    interruptions for childbirth 47–8
    parenting and mobility 45–50
childcare 13, 79–81
    at preschool stage 81–3
    cafeteria style benefits 90
    difficulties in finding suitable 62

financial benefits 90
information and referral service
    90–1
as a professional occupation 82
public provision 15
responsibility 79–81, 97
for school-aged children 84
and social policy 171–2
who stays at home in a crisis
    84–7
childcare advisors 91
childcare allowances 90
childcare assistance, workplace
    crèches 72
childcare consortia 89
childcare facilities, in homes for
    the elderly 92
childcare provision, lack of 46–7,
    58, 168
childcare vouchers 90
childlessness, voluntary 48–9
childminders 83
children
    decision to have 45–50
    effects of maternal employment
        on 77–9
    planning for 50
cognitive reappraisal 153–4
communication styles, sex
    differences 109–10, 115
commuter marriages 43–5
compromise, and problem solving
    42–3
concessions, asking for 63–4
coping strategies 28–33
counselling, for dual-career
    families 166–7

daycare centres, company 92
delegation 140–1
demographic changes 14–15
disabled people 12
  care for 172
division of labour, establishing
  attitudes to 38–9
domestic commitments, taboo
  against discussing 132
domestic overload, spillover 97–8
domestic work
  male participation 101–2
  responsibility for 96–100
  sharing 36
dual-career couples
  and anti-nepotism policies 160
  recruitment 160–1
  and relocation policies 161–2
dual-career marriage
  advantages of an egalitarian
    106–8
  preparing for 36–45
dual-earner family 12
  childcare arrangements 81–4
  problems facing 14–17
  responsibility for childcare
    79–81
  sharing, theory and practices 12,
    36
  transition to parenthood 57–73
  types 12

economic need 11
elderly, care for the 87–8, 92–3, 172
employee assistance and
    counselling programmes
    (EAPs) 166
employees, ideal 13, 17
employer attitudes, prejudice to
    returning mothers 47
energy, in new parenthood 74–5
equal opportunities
  at work and at home 114, 173–4
  legislation 15
  monitoring programmes 165–6
  and organisational effectiveness
    16–17

and part-time work 173–4
  policies 16, 114
Equal Opportunities Commission
  149–50
equal pay legislation 168
equality, in dual-career marriage
  106–8
equity, concept of 100–2
ethnic minorities 12
Europe, British policy compared
  with 15
European Commission 168
expectations 20, 23, 58, 59, 80

family friendly policies 114
family income, earnings gap for
  women 102–6
family patterns, traditional 12
family patterns, see also dual-
  earner family
fathers
  involvement with children 11
  mental health 81
  see also paternity leave
financial dependence 103–6
flexibility 13, 24–5, 120
flexible working year 121–2
flexiplace 122–4
flexitime 120–2
flexitour 121
freelance work 66, 124–5

gender attitudes 11
gender awareness training 114–15
gender roles 38–9
  renegotiating with parenthood
    59–60
gender stereotypes 20
  eliminating 163
  and homemaker mothers 78
  impact on job search and choice
    of location 40–2
  managers 108–10
  and misunderstandings at work
    110–12
  in organisations 108–10
glidingtime 121

guilt 32, 38, 46, 62, 76–7, 83, 87

handicapped children, childcare
    provision 86–7, 87
homemaker mothers, and sex
    stereotypes 78
homeworking 123–4

inflexibility, and schedule
    incompatibility 24–5
'intentionally childfree women'
    see childlessness, voluntary
interviews
    avoiding discrimination at 163
    dealing with personal questions
        at 150
irrational beliefs, questioning 155

job satisfaction
    and marital satisfaction 60
    spillover 27–8
job search
    dual-career couples 39–40
        stress and satisfaction in 42
job sharing 62, 125, 142–3

leave
    for family reasons 36, 171
    to care for the elderly 92–3
    see also maternity leave; parental
        leave; paternity leave
lifelines exercise 135
location, choice
    alternating decisions 43
    for dual-career couples 39,
        40–2
    when both partners are already
        established in jobs 42
    and relocation 160–2

male work ethic 13–14, 80–1
    challenging the 159
    and occupational stress 19–22
    parenting styles 69, 74
management styles, feminine
    characteristics 27
management training 132–3

managers
    attitudes 12, 13–14, 70
    gender stereotypes 108–10
    as role models 34, 133
marital relationships, role
    renegotiation strategy 148–9
marital satisfaction 106–8
    and job satisfaction 60
'maternal deprivation' (Bowlby)
    77–8
maternal employment, effects on
    children 77–9
maternity leave 15, 57, 58
    impact on parenting patterns
        80
    improvement 168–9
    length of 60–1
    paid 126–7
    problems after 64–6
maxiflex 121
meditation 155–6
men, with back-up at home 13,
    20–2
mission statement 159
mobility
    parenting and careers 45–50
    stress of 50–3
    using assertive skills in
        decisions 147–8
motherhood, delaying 47–8
'motherhood mandate' 76
mothers
    employed, mental health 58–9
    role conflict 75–7
    tiredness 74–5
'mother's helps' 82
mothers returning to work 58–9,
    62–3
    accumulation after leave 66
    changes in nature of the job 64–6
    reinstatement problems 64

nannies 82, 83, 88
needs assessment 129
    questionnaire 176–9
network groups, of women after
    maternity leave 127

nurseries 83
  and local government 89–90
  private 88
  state 172

occupational stress, and the male
    work ethic 19–22
off-site employment 123
opportunities for women 70–1,
    162–7
Opportunity 2000 16, 159
organisational climate 33–4
  professional behaviour 116
organisations
  changing 158–75
  help in career development
    issues 54–5
  help in childcare provision
    88–92
  help with eldercare 92–3
  help in facilitating the transition
    to parenthood 70–2
  help with gender stereotyping
    at work 114–16
  help in relieving stress 33–4
  men and women in 108–10
  policies and wider societal
    changes 167–71
overload
  dealing with 139–40
  recognising 137–9
  strategies for reducing 140–3

parent education 92
parental leave 15, 127
  pressure for legislation 169–71
parenthood
  dilemmas and issues for new
    parents 59–68
  informal policies 68–9
  transition to 57–9
    easing 126–9
parenting
  careers and mobility 45–50
  delaying decisions 47–8
  shared 59–60, 80–1
    advantages of 81

parenting seminars 92
parents, lack of support for new
    66–8
part-time work 124–5, 142
  choosing 29
  and equality of opportunity
    173–4
  to ease mothers returning 65
partnership deeds, maternity
    clause 127
passive responses 144, 145
paternity leave 127, 169
  paid 15
pensioners, services for 93
personal effectiveness training
    71–2, 133–4
play schemes 84
policy issues 168–71
preschool children, childcare
    arrangements 81–3
prioritising 30, 139–40
problem solving, and compromise
    42–3
professional women, part-time
    work 124–5
promotional policies 164

recruitment policies 54, 160
relatives, help with childcare 83
relaxation 155–6
relocation 13, 147–8
  company policy modifications
    54–5
  as a couple 52–3
  and location 160–2
  refusal 51–2
  stress of 50–3
respite care 93
role conflict, coping with 135–7
role cycling 134
role models 164
  employed mothers 38–9, 129
  lack for shared parenting 80
  management 34, 133
role redefinition 136–7

sabbaticals 126

schedule incompatibility, and
    inflexibility 24–5
school holidays 84, 92
schools, expectations of parents'
    availability 84
self-employed women 127
self-talk, constructive 153–4 Table
    8.3
sex roles
    changing 11
    dual roles, simultaneous or
        sequential 32
    spillover to work 112–14
sex stereotypes see gender
    stereotypes
sexism, countering at work 149–50
sexual discrimination
    affirmative action 173
    against married women 40–1
    countering at work 149–50
    legislation 168, 173
sexual harassment 112–14
    policy on 115
sexuality, at work 112–14
sick children 85–6
    alternative arrangements for 91
    leave to care for 86, 171
    paid leave for 15, 91
single mothers 12
social policy, and childcare 171–2
social support, for new parents 71
spillover 25–8
    of behaviour and attitudes from
        work to family 26–7
    coping with 31–3
    and domestic overload 97–8
    of stress and satisfaction 27–8
    of work into family time 26–7,
        34
statutory rights 15
stress 14
    and coping at work 19–35
    illnesses related to 26
    spillover 27–8
stress audits 33
stress management training 34,
    150–6

stress producing behaviour,
    recognising and modifying
    152–3
superwoman myth, challenging
    the 141
switching off 32

telecommuting 123–4
term-time working contracts 92
time, and energy, parenthood
    74–5
time management 29–30, 34,
    151–2
    balance sheet 151–2
    as a couple 30–1
tiredness, in new mothers 74–5
training and development
    132–57
transcendental meditation (TM)
    155–6
trust 34, 70
type A behaviour 27, 33, 119
    recognising and modifying
    152–3
type B behaviour 27

V-time 125
variable day 121
voluntary reduced time see V-time

weekend, extended 121
women
    corporate training for 164
    employed 11, 13
    professional development 32
        role conflict 32
    as the 'weaker sex' 110–12
women returners 126–9
    re-entry schemes 128
    retainer schemes 128
work overload 22–4
work week, compressed 121
work-family conflict 24–5
work-family issues, training in
    anticipation 133–5
work-family management
    training 135–56

workaholic syndrome 22–4, 119
    questioning the 28–9, 33–4,
        158–9
workforce, changing 11–12
working contracts, term-time 92
working from home 62, 122–3,
    142
working hours
    control over 26, 34, 70, 120–4
    long 13, 22–4

questioning the need for 28–9,
    140
reducing 124–6, 126
working together 96–118
    generating family income 102–6
    in the home 96–100
workplace, changing, reasons for
    14–17
workplace crèches 72, 83
    cost effectiveness 88–9